By the same author:

THE TUNNEL UNDER THE CHANNEL
THE RELAXED SELL

ALONE THROUGH THE DARK SEA

ALONE THROUGH THE DARK SEA

Thomas Whiteside

GEORGE BRAZILLER · NEW YORK

The first two chapters of this book
appeared originally in *The New Yorker*

GEORGE BRAZILLER, INC.
215 Park Avenue South
New York 3, N. Y.

FIRST PRINTING
Library of Congress Catalog Card Number: 64-21766

PRINTED IN THE UNITED STATES OF AMERICA

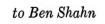

to Ben Shahn

Contents

FOREWORD

Each of the three stories in this book centers around the behavior of voyagers in isolation.

The first deals with the behavior of a man, Captain Kurt Carlsen who, after his ship the Flying Enterprise was disabled in a North Atlantic hurricane and after he had ordered his crew to abandon her, chose to stay on with his vessel, day after day in raging seas, until the end.

The second concerns a little group of people, the inhabitants of the tiny South Atlantic island of Tristan da Cunha. The uniquely Arcadian existence of these islanders, who are in large part the descendants of shipwrecked mariners, who speak English in the ancient accents of Wellington's troops, and who up to recent times have inhabited one of the loneliest outposts in the world, was shattered when a volcano rose up, erupted on the edge of their thatched-roof settlement, and forced them off their island home and into a bewildering period of exile in England.

The third story deals, not with an individual or with a group of people, but with a machine voyaging in isolation; it is a step-by-step account of the journey of the unmanned spacecraft Mariner 2 through the void of space from Earth to the planet Venus.

Each of these stories involves a dramatic adventure, but it is not only with adventure that I have been concerned in writing this book. It is, rather, the change in our perspective that a detailed view of life or movement under conditions of extreme isolation affords us—the opportunity to see, in such unusual situations, a standard by which we may judge our own behavior and our own outlook.

T. W

A Powerful Sense Of His Duty

Of all the winter storms to sweep the North Atlantic in recent years, few are more sorely remembered by seafaring people and the inhabitants of many European coastal areas than the gales that prevailed over the eastern part of the ocean during the last few days of 1951. The area of disturbance extended from Scandinavia to the Iberian Peninsula, and even into North Africa—snow began falling one day during Christmas week at Maktar, Tunisia—and the storms stretched westward into the ocean for several hundred miles. A news dispatch from London that the New York *Times* printed on its front page on December 30th described the Atlantic as "one vast boiling cauldron, from the Bay of Biscay to Britain," and it went on to estimate at twenty-six the total number of people dead or missing in the storms—an estimate that was to rise to sixty before the year was out. Winds within the storm area were said to be blowing at full hurricane force.

Ships were in distress everywhere. Even the largest

ocean liners had a terrible time of it; when the Queen Mary, badly knocked about, arrived in Southampton seventy-two hours late, Captain Harry Grattidge, her skipper, told the press that the voyage to New York and back was the worst he had known since 1914. "There was no other word for the seas but terrific," he was quoted as saying. The skippers of many smaller vessels found the seas disastrous. The Norwegian tanker Osthav buckled amidships and broke in two off the Spanish coast, near Coruña; the German freighter Irene Oldendorff went down off the North Sea island of Borkum with a loss of twenty-two lives; and the Dutch coastal steamer Gemma was driven aground near Biarritz and her eight-man crew was drowned. These and many other maritime casualties were faithfully reported in this country during the dying days of December; occurring, as they did, in the midst of the festive season, they provided the safely landlocked public with a chilling inventory of the ferocities of nature and of the perils endured by those who made their living on the high seas.

Of all the manifold adversities brought on by the storms, none attracted such intense interest here and throughout the world as the plight of a United States freighter named the Flying Enterprise. The American public began to hear about the Flying Enterprise on December 29th, when press dispatches from Europe reported that several ships in the eastern Atlantic had picked up an emergency radio message from the freighter to the effect that she was encountering hurricane conditions some three hundred and thirty miles southwest of Cape Clear, on the southern tip of Ireland; that she was "just drifting," with a heavy list; and that her situation was grave. The significance of this last phrase was underlined by the additional information that the Flying Enterprise had fifty-one people aboard —ten passengers in addition to her master and her crew of forty. By the following day, the storms were at their worst over most of the eastern Atlantic, and it became apparent that the gravity of the freighter's position had deepened into desperation; the press reported that the passengers and crew had been ordered to abandon ship, and that they, along with the body of one passenger who had drowned, had been picked up by boats from rescue ships.

While these events were dramatic, what really focused attention on the Flying Enterprise, as distinct from the many other ships in difficulties at the time, was the news that her captain had chosen to remain aboard after ordering everybody else off, and that (as the *Times* put it), having "stubbornly resisted repeated attempts to rescue him," he was sticking to his ship—now heeled over at a sixty-to-eighty-degree angle—with the expressed determination to keep command of her as long as she remained afloat, or at least until a tug took her safely in tow. The name of the captain, a thirty-seven-year-old native of Denmark who was currently a resident of Woodbridge, New Jersey, was Henrik Kurt Carlsen—a name that was to become familiar throughout the world over the next two weeks.

The story of Carlsen's unremitting efforts to save the Flying Enterprise, relayed to the public in day-by-day installments in the press and over the air, was enough to excite anybody's imagination—how he held out aboard his wallowing ship for thirteen days and nights, the first six of them alone and the rest in the company of the young mate of a British rescue tug who had joined him on board; how, alone or with the aid of his young companion, he managed, time after time, to haul towlines onto the Flying Enterprise, only to have them part in rough seas; how, having surmounted these and other obstacles, he and his helper kept the ship under tow toward the Cornish port of Falmouth, until, with a safe harbor tantalizingly close, a new storm arose and the ship went down; and how he and the mate jumped from her funnel before she disappeared and were picked up by an attending tug.

It was a heartbreaking climax to a drama that had all but pushed the war in Korea off the front pages for almost a fortnight, and public sympathy for Carlsen over the loss of his ship was exceeded only by the universally expressed admiration for his courage and resourcefulness in attempting to save her. He was welcomed in Falmouth with flowers, speeches, and cheers; New York gave him an enthusiastic ticker-tape reception; and medals and citations for bravery were pressed upon him by Congress and the governments of many other countries. All sorts of commercial offers were pressed upon him, too, and if he had accepted them, he would have become wealthy overnight. But Carlsen did not accept them; he refused to cash in on his popularity. "I only did my duty as a simple seaman," he explained. He seemed like a hero from another time.

The Flying Enterprise began her final voyage on December 21, 1951, when she left Hamburg for New York. She was a seven-year-old vessel of 6,711 tons—a wartime C-1 freighter, slightly smaller and slower than a Victory ship—which the Isbrandtsen Company, a relatively small but well-known and aggressive cargo line, had bought from the United States Maritime Commission in 1947. She had two decks in her superstructure—the topmost bridge deck, which contained the officers' quarters and the radio room, and the cabin deck, where the passengers were quartered. Isbrandtsen had had her on the European run for some three years, carrying general cargo and a small number of passengers, and now, as she headed down the Elbe for the North Sea under Carlsen's command, she was lightly loaded, to about a third of her carrying capacity, with a typical assortment of freight. In addition to her principal burden— twelve hundred and seventy tons of pig iron, which had been loaded in Rotterdam—her holds contained four hundred and eighty-six tons of coffee, seven hundred bales of peat moss, twelve Volkswagens, three hundred and ninety-three barrels of bone meal, twenty-five barrels of onions and gherkins, three tons of bird cages, a hundred and twenty-five bales of animal hair, five tons of carpets, sixty tons of graphite, four hundred and forty-seven tons of rags, a number of German-made typewriters, a further number of antiques, a load of mail and express packages, and a hundred and twenty-five sections of steel pipe. She also carried, on her main deck, fore and aft, dozens of bags of naphthalene—the stuff of which mothballs are made— placed there so as not to contaminate the cargo in the holds.

To her captain, the route to New York was a comfortably familiar one. Carlsen, a short, stocky man with a pleasant, rather boyish face, was an experienced sailor for his age, having spent twenty-three of his thirty-seven years at sea. The son of a Jack-of-all-trades from Hillerød, he began his career at fourteen as a cook's helper aboard a Danish schooner engaged in the grain trade, worked for a couple of years as a deckhand and sailmaker aboard other big Danish sailing vessels, and then, after a stint in the Danish Navy, carried on in the Danish Merchant Marine as an able seaman and, later, as a junior officer. In 1938, when he was second officer of the Danish freighter Sessa, he married a Jutland girl, Agnes Sorensen, and shortly afterward, when his ship was assigned to a regular run between Chilean ports and New York, he brought his bride over here to live; during the war years, when he took out American citizenship papers, he sailed as chief mate and master of various ships in the United States Merchant Marine that belonged to or were chartered by the Isbrandtsen line. He had skippered the Flying Enterprise for most of the time that Isbrandtsen had had her on the European run, and this voyage was to be his forty-fourth crossing of the Atlantic as her master.

The Flying Enterprise was due in New York on January 3rd; aside from a fog that further slowed the freighter's normally slow and cautious progress down the Elbe, Carlsen had no special indications that the voyage ahead would be an abnormally rough one for early winter, or that the arrival of the ship at her destination was likely to be seriously delayed. An abundant Christmas table was promised for everybody on board, and while Carlsen would have been happy if the ship's schedule had permitted him to spend the holidays with his family in Woodbridge, he was looking forward to longer-than-usual chats with them by short-wave radio, since he was an enthusiastic and skillful amateur radio operator and kept a private transmitter in his cabin. As a treat for his passengers and crew, he had promised to allow them to talk to their families, too, at Christmas, via coöperative amateur radio operators near their homes.

There was to be little of such shipboard cheer. The Flying Enterprise continued to encounter heavy fog until she reached a point about halfway down the English Channel, and then, on December 24th, in the open sea, rough weather set in from the west. Conditions steadily worsened, and most of the passengers spent Christmas Day being thoroughly seasick, for the Flying Enterprise was taking a bad buffeting. Continual strong winds were now forecast for the area, and by December 26th both the wind and the seas had risen to such an extent that Carlsen—giving due regard to the miserable state of his passengers, most of whom were fairly elderly, as well as to the security of the Volkswagens in his cargo, which were stowed uncrated in one of the holds—decided that it would be wise to heave to and ride out the worst of the weather. He did so, heading the ship off the wind and keeping the propellers turning at the minimum rate necessary to maintain steerageway.

All that night, the Flying Enterprise lay pitching and rolling in very heavy seas. The velocity of the wind increased steadily, until it reached Force 12—the highest reading on Beaufort's scale of wind power, indicating hurricane-force winds of at least sixty-five miles an hour—and, as dawn approached, the waves breaking over the ship were between thirty and forty feet high. At about six-thirty in the morning, everybody on board was startled by an explosive snapping noise. Under the crashing seas, the ship's steel deck and hull plates had cracked in two places amidships. One fracture ran from a corner of No. 3 hatch to the port side and twelve feet down the hull; the other ran from the corner of the deckhouse to the starboard side and also twelve feet down the hull.

Carlsen immediately ordered all hands on deck, and put a gang to work on the fractured area. Cracked plates were nothing new to a seaman of his experience, and although he knew that the damage was serious, he felt confident that he could bring the ship and her passengers safely into port. To ease the strain on the fore part of the vessel, Carlsen kept her headed well off the wind. During the morning, his deck gang, working in seas that broke heavily and constantly over the foredeck, toiled away at suturing the cracks. For this, they used the bitts—the steel mooring posts placed at intervals along a ship's deck—fore and aft of the cracks, lashing them together with wire hawsers to keep the cracks from widening. To help prevent water from entering the interior of the ship, Carlsen also had his men fill the cracks with concrete, and, in addition, he had them construct a breakwater across the deck forward of the fracture with some of the bags of naphthalene. When this work was completed, he dispatched a brief radio message to his owners reporting the incident and his position, which, because of wind and drift, was now some fifty miles north of his normal course. Although he knew that about the best he could do in the prevailing weather was to hold his own, he had already concluded that he would have to put in for repairs either at an English or French port or in the Azores.

On the night of December 27th, the wind and seas abated somewhat, and Carlsen, who had been on the bridge for seventy-five hours, was able to get a few hours' sleep in his cabin, on the starboard side of the bridge deck. The next morning, however, the ship ran into a new cyclonic storm. The wind increased to hurricane force, and the seas became the most violent in Carlsen's memory, with the exception of some he had been through in the Caribbean during the notorious hurricane of 1938. The waves that now bore down upon the Flying Enterprise assumed dreadful size, and under their impact she rolled about more or less helplessly. Then, at about 11:30 A.M., she was hit broadside from starboard by a wave sixty feet high, which struck her a blow so jarring that it smashed the starboard lifeboat, ripped loose the steel furniture that was bolted to the floor in the passenger cabins, and even tossed the ship's compasses out of their binnacles. The crosstrees on the foremast disappeared in a solid mass of flying water.

Under the shuddering impact of the great wave, the Flying Enterprise was tossed over into the trough of the sea almost on her beam-ends, and instead of recovering and rolling back upright, she remained listing to port at an angle of about twenty-five degrees. Her cargo had shifted. In an attempt to right her, Carlsen immediately ordered the engines full ahead and the wheel hard right. The Flying Enterprise did not respond, so he ordered full ahead with a hard-left wheel. Again she failed to respond, and Carlsen requested his engine-room crew to check the steering gear. The chief engineer reported back that the steering controls appeared to be in order; the trouble was that the engines were inoperable, owing to a loss of lubricating oil caused by the list of the ship, and it would take hours to get them going again, if they could be started at all. Until then, the Flying Enterprise would be left helpless, wallowing and drifting at the mercy of the elements. Her list increased to thirty degrees.

It was at this point that Carlsen told his radio operator to send out the distress call that the press here reported on December 29th. The call consisted of what is known as an urgency signal—a series of three "X"s tapped out on the telegraphic key and representing not an SOS but an urgent notification that the signalling vessel is in serious difficulties. The signal was followed by a message summarizing the situation aboard the Flying Enterprise and requesting other ships in the vicinity to indicate their positions. In the meantime, Carlsen had ordered his dazed and frightened passengers—none of whom, miraculously, had been injured by the shattering smash from starboard—to put on life jackets and assemble in one of the passageways on the cabin deck; now he asked them to keep themselves as warm as they could and to conserve their strength, because it might be necessary for them to leave the ship.

A number of vessels quickly responded to the urgency signal. At three o'clock that afternoon, Carlsen, having been told by his chief engineer that there was no hope of getting the engines going again, and seeing the ship's list gradually increase, changed his urgency signal to a full SOS, and several ships in the vicinity immediately changed course and headed, through terrible seas and in winds that sometimes reached ninety miles an hour, for the Flying Enterprise. They included the British freighters Sheridan, Sherborne, and War Hawk; the United States freighter Southland; the German freighter Arion; the Norwegian tanker Westfal Larsen; and the United States Navy transport General A. W. Greely.

None of them reached the disabled ship before the approach of darkness, and rescue operations had to be put off until early the next morning. By that time, the Flying Enterprise had increased her list to sixty degrees—and eighty degrees in rolls—and to those aboard the assisting ships gathered at the scene, she appeared to be about ready to go under. Occasionally, she heeled over so far that she shipped water through her funnel. Although the weather had moderated considerably overnight, it was still very severe—so rough that during the ensuing rescue operations, five lifeboats from the assisting ships were knocked out of action. One lifeboat sent from the Sherborne foundered; two more—one from the War Hawk and the other from the Westfal Larsen—capsized; a fourth, from the Greely, was carried against the hull of the Southland when its motor failed, and damaged both itself and the fifth, one of the Southland's own lifeboats, which lay alongside.

As for the Flying Enterprise's own two lifeboats, both were out of commission, the starboard boat having been smashed by the sea on the previous day and the port boat being unusable, in Carlsen's judgment, because of the list of the ship. Since it was impossible for the lifeboats from the rescue ships to come alongside the Flying Enterprise, there was no way for those aboard to leave except by jumping into the sea. Carlsen therefore ordered the passengers to the port rail of the bridge deck, and, while lifeboats from the rescue vessels closed in and the tanker Westfal Larsen circled around pumping hundreds of tons of oil overboard to moderate the waves, they began jumping one by one, each accompanied by a crew member. Then came the turn of the rest of the crew—except for a group of volunteers—and they jumped in groups of five, at first from amidships and then, when that position seemed too dangerous because of the rolling of the ship, from the stern. Most of the castaways and the body of one casualty, a stateless man named Bunjakowski, who was drowned with his pet dog, were picked up by boats from the Greely; the rest were hauled aboard the boats of the Southland, the Arion, and the Westfal Larsen.

While this complicated and perilous lifesaving operation was going on, the masters of the attending ships, naturally enough, were in no position to concern themselves with the fate of the Flying Enterprise as a ship; in any case, her condition appeared to be hopeless. On the previous day, however, her owners had arranged for a Dutch salvage tug to head for the ship from a position some seven hundred miles away, in the Bay of Biscay, and at the time the rescue operations started, Carlsen had hope, despite the desperate plight of his vessel, that she would remain afloat long enough for the tug to get her in tow. It was on the basis of this hope that the volunteers had stayed aboard the ship to help secure the tow. But when the rescue operations drew to a close and all the rest of the crew had been picked up by lifeboats, Carlsen informed the volunteers that, considering the condition of the ship, he could not take the responsibility for risking their lives, and ordered them to jump overboard after the others. They did so, and were picked up by a lifeboat from the Greely.

"After all were in the boat, I asked the first officer of the Enterprise, Mr. Bartak, where the captain was, and he informed me that the captain would not leave his ship," the officer in charge of the lifeboat wrote later, in an official report. "I again questioned him carefully about this, and still received the same answer. I had no choice but to head back to the Greely. As we passed to windward of the Enterprise, I saw the captain standing on the boat deck aft, and we all waved to him."

As the last lifeboat pulled away from the Flying Enterprise, Carlsen, exhausted though he was, at once turned to the preparations necessary for carrying on his lonely watch aboard the shattered hulk. One of his first tasks was to look to his means of communicating with the rescue vessels that remained standing by. Because the tremendous sea that had struck the ship had knocked out the electric generators, the Flying Enterprise was without light, without heat, and without power, and one result of this power failure was that the ship's big regular one-kilowatt transmitter, in the radio cabin, on the port side of the bridge deck, was useless, as was Carlsen's own amateur one-kilowatt transmitter, which he kept in his cabin, on the starboard side. The radio cabin also contained a fifty-watt battery-powered Morse transmitter, but since the batteries were running low (the set had been in almost continuous use since the failure of the ship's generators, and as the ship's list increased, some of the acid had spilled out of the batteries), Carlsen decided to reserve the use of this set for the most dire kind of emergency; he rigged it so that if he should be forced to leave the radio room in a hurry, he could instantly jam the Morse key to keep the set producing a continuous signal on the international distress wave length.

In his own cabin, he dug out from among his amateur equipment a little five-watt battery-powered voice transmitter, which he had bought some time before for use in a small cabin cruiser his father-in-law had built. Using a length of the electric cord from his desk lamp and an oar from the smashed lifeboat, he rigged up a makeshift antenna and stuck it out of one of the portholes of his cabin, which were now nearly overhead. Considering its tiny power and the limitations of its jury rig, the transmitter functioned remarkably well. Carlsen got in touch with the Greely and methodically set up arrangements for future communications, including radio contacts at prescribed intervals; he also requested the Greely to continue standing by until the arrival of the Dutch tug, and to continue relaying, as she had been doing for some twenty-four hours, radio messages between the Flying Enterprise and distant points—Isbrandtsen headquarters in New York, for example. During these and subsequent radio conversations, as Captain Neil Olsen, the master of the Greely, later told the press, Carlsen did not express the least anxiety about his ship but spoke with an air of calm cheerfulness.

As Carlsen's first day alone aboard his ship drew to a close, he was able to report to the Greely, before announcing his retirement for the night (his listeners were struck at the idea of a man's expecting to get any sleep under such conditions), that although his ship had been shipping tons of water in her cracked hold and was still listing at sixty-five degrees, with rolls to eighty degrees, she did not show signs of riding any lower. His principal concerns now appeared to be the weather prospects and the progress of the tug that was coming to his assistance.

Earlier, Carlsen had calculated on the basis of information supplied him by Isbrandtsen headquarters by way of the Greely that the tug would arrive not much more than forty-eight hours after the transfer of his passengers and crew. The name of the tug was the Oceaan, and it was the second tug of Dutch ownership—no British or French seagoing tugs could be obtained in that week of emergencies —that Isbrandtsen had tried to engage. The owners of the first Dutch tug, the Zwarte Zee, had got into a disagreement with Isbrandtsen over the hiring terms, and by the time that the terms were straightened out, the Zwarte Zee had already been engaged by another ship, the British freighter Angusbrae, which had lost her rudder and was lying helplessly off the coast of Portugal. Isbrandtsen then enlisted the services of the Oceaan, which immediately set out for the Flying Enterprise. At noon on December 31st, Carlsen informed his owners, via the Greely's radio, that the weather forecast was favorable and that the Oceaan was expected to arrive the following day.

But Carlsen was in for another setback. While the Oceaan was steaming toward the Flying Enterprise, the other Dutch tug, the Zwarte Zee, towing the distressed Angusbrae through heavy seas in the Bay of Biscay, was struck by the Danish freighter Bjoern Clausen, and suffered such serious damage that she herself had to send out an SOS call. Since the lives of the men aboard the Zwarte Zee were in danger and the Flying Enterprise was all but abandoned, the Oceaan was diverted to the assistance of the other tug, which she eventually managed to take in tow and bring into Saint-Nazaire. Carlsen was left to carry on alone without any definite prospect of help.

The Isbrandtsen people had to start hunting for a tug all over again, and later that day they informed Carlsen by radio that they had succeeded in engaging the services of the British eleven-hundred-and-thirty-six-ton Turmoil, which, with its four thousand horsepower, was, and still is, one of the most powerful tugs in the world. In the same message, Isbrandtsen gave Carlsen a new date for the estimated arrival of his desperately needed towing help—noon on January 1st—but once again the skipper was disappointed. The Turmoil, then towing the storm-damaged British tanker Mactra into Falmouth, was delayed by a break in the towline, and did not set out from Falmouth Roads until daylight of January 1st. It took her three days to reach Carlsen's ship.

In the six days and nights between the abandonment of the Flying Enterprise by her passengers and crew and the arrival of the Turmoil, Carlsen adapted himself to the hardships of life aboard his unheated, unlighted, and half-capsized ship with ready inventiveness and a kind of plodding orderliness. In addition to her permanent list of sixty-five degrees to port, the ship, with tons of water sloshing and booming around in her flooded No. 3 hold, lay with her head settled fairly well down, with her stern riding high in the air, and (although Carlsen never knew it until he was informed by one of the standby ships) with her rudderpost broken and the blade swinging free above the water. Of all the problems he constantly had to cope with, that of moving from one place to another about the ship was among the most difficult. When the last of the rescuing lifeboats departed on December 29th, he was left alone in a crazily inverted world, where what had been a deck now became a nearly upright bulkhead, and what had been a bulkhead now served as a deck—where once level passageways across the ship became steeper than a sharply pitched house roof and, moreover, heaved and lurched in a wild, unpredictable fashion. Under these circumstances, the negotiation of even a relatively short distance was extremely hazardous and physically exhausting, but such excursions were frequently necessary for inspecting various parts of the ship, for obtaining supplies, and for maintaining communication with the outside world.

On his first day alone, Carlsen decided to make his headquarters not in the captain's quarters, on the starboard, or high, side of the bridge deck—the only deck not partly awash—but in the radio operator's cabin, on the port, or low, side, where, in the event of further emergency, he could quickly jam the key that would start the continuing distress signal on the ship's auxiliary radio. This living arrangement itself cost him a great deal of effort, for in order to get to his own cabin and its voice transmitter, he had to slide downhill and out the door of the radio cabin, turn to the right, make his way along a passageway so tilted from side to side that he had nothing but the trough of a V as a foothold, turn right again and pull himself by a handrail up a transverse passageway, just aft of the wheelhouse, to the door of his cabin. To keep to his radio schedule, he had to make the round trip six times a day.

At night, he slept in the radio cabin. The bunk installed there was on the high side of the room and, of course, impossible to use; to make a relatively level place to sleep, Carlsen collected blankets and pillows from nearby cabins, wedged them into the V-shaped angle made by a built-in settee and the bulkhead on the low side, and stretched a mattress over them. It was cold and wet—the cabin was unprotected from the chilling wind and spray, because he could not risk being hindered by any closed doors if the ship should begin to founder, and his clothes were thoroughly soaked from his frequent trips on the open deck —but Carlsen slept as long as he could, since, as he later remarked, he was determined to get enough sleep to keep in good physical condition.

Within a few hours after the rescue of his passengers and crew, Carlsen began to get hungry and thirsty. After rising the next morning and making the first day's scheduled radio contacts with the Greely, he set off on a foraging expedition into the reeling interior of the deckhouse. Climbing, crawling, and slithering around in semi-darkness, he at last reached the ship's dry-storage room, on the main deck. After getting its steel door open and floundering around among the chaotically jumbled contents, he managed to extract a large doughnut-shaped poundcake that the cook had prepared for the New Year's celebration. As he was getting out the poundcake, a big can of tomato juice fell on him from above, and he decided to take that along, too. Because he needed both hands to get himself up to the radio cabin again, he thrust his arm through the hole in the center of the poundcake and carried it as though he were wearing a huge mangle; as for the can of tomato juice, he moved it along by kicking and dribbling it, like a soccer player. The poundcake lasted Carlsen a good many days, but the tomato juice was soon gone, leaving him once more short of liquid; owing to the failure of the ship's hydraulic-pressure system, none of the faucets on the ship produced any water. Carlsen remedied this situation by further excursions to the ship's dry-storage room, which produced a number of quart bottles of beer.

Besides being without heat, Carlsen was in need of light—his flashlight had disappeared, probably washed overboard—but he was able to solve the latter problem readily enough. Rummaging around in his own cabin, he came up with a few candles and a set of holders with pins attached to them—the kind sometimes stuck into cakes for festive occasions. They had been casually given to him in Hamburg, just before the ship sailed, by a fellow amateur radio operator and his wife, who had thought they might add a decorative touch to the skipper's Christmas table. From then on, Carlsen had light in the radio cabin at night whenever he wanted it. He would jab the spiked holder into the mattress of his makeshift bunk, and then, as the wind howled outside the open door and his light burned fitfully in the chilly, wet drafts, he would read before going to sleep. His reading matter consisted of one book—"The Law of

Seamen," by Martin J. Norris, a standard guide to admiralty law for seafaring men.

As the days of waiting passed and a succession of U.S. Navy ships carried on the task of standing by the Flying Enterprise—the Greely was relieved on January 1st by the Navy supply ship Golden Eagle, which, in turn, was relieved on January 2nd by the destroyer John W. Weeks —Carlsen continued to subsist on his diet of poundcake and beer, and doggedly kept up an exhausting daily routine of inspecting the fractures on the foredeck and incessantly climbing, crawling, scrambling, and sliding between the radio cabin and his voice transmitter in the captain's cabin. He also systematically occupied himself with other work, such as assembling as many of the ship's records as he could, among them payroll documents and his officers' maritime-license certificates, which he removed from their frames on the bulkhead of a passageway. He even recorded the amounts of money deductible from various officers' and crew members' pay because of purchases from the ship's canteen. Some of these records he eventually placed in a watertight container that he lashed to two life jackets and threw overboard, to be picked up by the standby ship (this, however, was lost in the racing seas); certain other documents, such as the ship's log (which he faithfully kept up to date), the bridge log, and the ship's register, he put in a little handbag, with the intention of keeping them with him, sink or swim. (These documents, too, were eventually lost in the seas.)

In his regular radio contacts with the standby ship, which began at eight o'clock in the morning and continued at two-hour intervals until eight o'clock at night, Carlsen remained unfailingly optimistic about the outcome of his struggle to bring the Flying Enterprise into port, and impervious to all suggestions—including several from Hans Isbrandtsen, the president of the Isbrandtsen Company—that he place his own safety above his concern for his ship. As an old mariner with considerable respect for the traditions of the sea, Isbrandtsen was unwilling to undercut Carlsen's authority as a ship's master by giving him orders at sea, but as soon as he learned that Carlsen was remaining aboard alone, he sent off a message firmly informing him that no useful purpose could be served by his risking—or even, as he put it, sacrificing—his life, and going on to "recommend" strongly that Carlsen transfer to the Greely. To this, Carlsen replied merely with a request that his employers dictate to him, in plain language, the terms under which he should permit a tow to be connected ("NO CONTRACTS AVAILABLE HERE"), adding, almost casually, "WILL OF COURSE STAY WITH VESSEL UNTIL PORT IS REACHED OR SHE GOES DOWN."

  With equal resolution, he rejected a subsequent proposal that he be transferred, on a purely temporary basis, to the standby ship pending the arrival of the tug, and in a radio conversation he had on New Year's Day with Captain William E. Donohue, master of the Golden Eagle, he explained, in a rather pedantic manner, "We captains when entrusted with a large amount of dollars' worth of cargo and mail should look after them as being our responsibility. We cannot go away and leave it." He went on to dictate one of the several messages of greeting that he sent to his wife and children. In the early-morning hours of January 2nd, as the Golden Eagle, having been relieved by the Weeks, prepared to steam away, he said to Captain Donohue, in a final, unscheduled radio contact, "Goodbye, Captain. Everything is all right. There is nothing new, nothing exciting. I'm getting a little lonesome but kind of getting used to it now. I am sorry this has upset your schedule—you have lost a couple of days." Then he slid and scrambled back down the nearly upright passageway to the radio cabin, to his poundcake and beer, and to further hours of earnest perusal, under the flickering light of his candle, of "The Law of Seamen."

Carlsen says he does not remember having any special reason for reading "The Law of Seamen." "I just thought it would make constructive reading for me," he once remarked. There seems little doubt, however, that in continuing to stick with his ship, which he was convinced he could bring into port, he was preserving her status under the maritime laws governing salvage, which he might have jeopardized if he had stepped off her even temporarily. The legal problem that seems to have been worrying Carlsen was not whether his ship might become a sort of "free prize" of the sea if he left her—the concept of the "free prize," although widely held among laymen, does not exist in admiralty law—but, rather, what kind of salvage claims might be levelled against her owners if she were to reach port under tow.

There are two general types of ship salvage—contract salvage and pure salvage. In contract salvage, the salvor carries out the job under a contractural arrangement with the owner of the ship or his representative, who may be the insurance underwriter or the ship's captain; in pure salvage, a derelict ship is taken into port, usually with the consent of the owner but sometimes without it, and the charge for the job becomes akin to a lien on the ship. Contract salvage is carried out under several kinds of arrangement: the whole job may be done on a flat-fee basis; or the owner, the insurance underwriter, or the captain may hire a tug by the hour or day, without further reward; or the tug may be contracted for without detailed discussion of the terms, which can later be negotiated privately or through arbitration or a court decree; or the tug's services may be obtained under the contractual principle known as "no cure, no pay," by which the shipowner loses nothing if the salvage attempt is unsuccessful and the salvor, if successful, stands to gain, through subsequent arbitration or court action, a fee commensurate with the size of his gamble.

In response to Carlsen's message asking for the terms of a suitable towing contract, Isbrandtsen informed the skipper that the Turmoil had been hired on a no-cure, no-pay basis. With knowledge of such a contract and of the legal protection inherent in it, another skipper in Carlsen's position might now have felt free to seek safety on an escort vessel without fear of losing his full rights in the ship or of leaving her prey to any unwelcome salvor. (A ship's master has the right to reject offered salvage.) Carlsen nevertheless stayed where he was.

On January 2nd, via the Golden Eagle, he sent a message to Isbrandtsen saying, "SITUATION MORNING OF THE SECOND. NUMBER THREE HOLD FULL OF WATER. ENGINE ROOM TAKING SOME WATER HOWEVER NOT MUCH. DECKS AWASH TO HATCH COAMINGS PORT SIDE BUT CHANCES ARE GOOD THAT SHE WILL STAY AFLOAT. LIST ABOUT 65 DEGREES. OTHERWISE CONDITIONS UNCHANGED. WILL TRANSFER TO TUG WHEN CONTRACT IS SIGNED SATISFACTORILY AND LINES ARE FAST." And he added, "ALL YOUR MESSAGES HAVE BEEN RECEIVED BY ME. PLEASE NOTIFY MY FAMILY I AM WELL AND HAVE SUFFICIENT PROVISIONS." Later that day, after the Weeks had made three unsuccessful attempts to pass food and supplies to him by line across very rough seas, Carlsen managed to provide himself with something hot to drink—for the first time in five days. Collecting a quart or so of water from what was left in the thermos flasks in the passenger cabins below, he poured a cupful into the empty tomato-juice can and patiently held the can over a sprig of three or four candles stuck into his mattress until at last the water came to a boil. Then, with a tea bag he had obtained from the dry-storage room, he brewed himself a cup of tea.

The Turmoil arrived in the vicinity of the Flying Enterprise at about 11 P.M. on January 3rd. As she approached the casualty in the dim moonlight that occasionally broke through heavy clouds, her crew could see no signs of life aboard the darkened hulk, but when the Turmoil had come within a few hundred yards of her, they saw the play of a flashlight on the after bridge deck. The flashlight was one of the few supplies that the Weeks had finally succeeding in passing to Carlsen by line during the day, and, using it, the captain was making his way to a point at the stern rail on the main deck where he might receive a heaving line from the tug.

Several hours earlier, Carlsen had held a three-way radio conversation with Captain William L. Thompson, the commander of the Weeks, and Captain Dan Parker, the master of the Turmoil, to discuss arrangements for connecting a towline, and it had been agreed among them that the Flying Enterprise would be towed from the stern, rather than from the bow, in order to shield the low-lying forward hatches from the heavy westerly seas. Because connecting a towline aboard a ship listing as heavily as the

Flying Enterprise is a tricky affair, requiring very heavy labor, Captain Parker had estimated that he would need to get about twelve experienced men aboard the casualty to handle towropes and tackle, but as he got close to the Flying Enterprise it became clear that such a transfer would be far too dangerous to attempt, either by day or by night, in the prevailing conditions. Carlsen told Captain Parker that he intended to attempt to take a line aboard alone, and without waiting for daylight.

Customarily, the procedure for getting a towline aboard a manned ship from a tug is for the tug to throw over a light, half-inch heaving line, to which are attached a series of successive heavier lines, known as messengers, and, finally, the towline itself, a wire rope about two inches in diameter. However, hauling in four or five hundred feet of two-inch wire rope was obviously impossible for one man, and it was decided that the Turmoil would use a modified procedure. She would send over a heaving line to which was attached a length of messenger line looped double all the way back to the tug; the eye of this loop would then be hooked around one of the bitts at the stern of the Flying Enterprise, and the tug, now in possession of something like an endless line controlled by her winches, would draw heavier and heavier lines around the bitts until the towline itself arrived and Carlsen could make it fast.

In conformity with this plan, Carlsen stationed himself at the starboard, or high, rail at the stern, and at about midnight the Turmoil was maneuvered into a position from which a heaving line could be flung over to him. Owing to the fact that the disabled ship had a sixty-five-degree list, and to the fact that the Flying Enterprise and the Turmoil were drifting around in the heavy swell at different speeds, and to the further fact that Carlsen was under a severe handicap—he could not let go of the rail to pick up the heaving line without being in danger of sliding down the drenched and oily deck into the sea, which left him only one hand free for catching—the job of getting the heaving line to him was a frustrating business. But after three unsuccessful attempts had been made, Carlsen caught it. Hauling the line in to give himself some slack, he had almost managed to get it around one of the starboard bitts when a wave carried the Turmoil away and the line snapped.

All the next day, from eight o'clock in the morning until the middle of the afternoon, in mounting seas and a thirty-five-mile-an-hour wind, attempts were made to get a line fast on the Flying Enterprise. It was exhausting and dangerous work for Carlsen, and also tedious work for the crew of the tug. Every time the heaving line fell back into the sea, the tug had to back away to avoid fouling its propellers, the crew had to rerig the line, and Captain Parker had to maneuver the tug into position all over again. Eventually, on his seventh try, Carlsen managed to catch and retain the heaving line. This time, he was also able to haul in the doubled one-inch messenger line and loop it around the bitts. The Turmoil started her winches and began hauling successively heavier messenger lines around the bitts and back to the tug, until the steel towline itself appeared out of the water, wound itself around the bitts, and started back to the tug. But then, just as it was about to be hauled on board the Turmoil, the messenger line pulling it gave way. The heavy steel hawser raced around the bitts on the Flying Enterprise in a shower of sparks, and plunged into the sea. The tow was lost.

It was well into the afternoon before the Turmoil could get back into position for another try, and the sea had become very rough. For once, this was a circumstance that worked in Carlsen's favor. As the Turmoil moved in close astern of the Flying Enterprise, a great wave lifted her and banged her against the freighter. In that instant of collision, the mate of the Turmoil, a twenty-seven-year-old Englishman from Hook Green, Kent, named Kenneth R. Dancy, impulsively leaped from the deck of the tug and caught hold of the stern rail of the Flying Enterprise not far from where Carlsen was hanging on. Reaching through the bars of the rail, he shook hands with Carlsen, who was wearing a blue-and-orange life jacket and who, despite his drenched and long-unshaven appearance, seemed in surprisingly fit condition. As Dancy recalls the moment, Carlsen said to him, "Welcome to the Flying Enterprise. Make yourself comfortable."

That evening, after efforts to connect a tow had been abandoned for the day, Carlsen explained to Dancy how he moved about on deck—in a sort of crouching, clinging, sidewise crawl— and then he led him slowly amidships and up into the captain's cabin, where he found a life jacket for the mate, since Dancy had leaped from the Turmoil without one. From the moment that he staggered into the housing of the crazily listing ship, Dancy (as he wrote some time later) was almost overcome by an oppressive claustrophobic feeling, which never entirely left him during his entire stay aboard the Flying Enterprise. This feeling was hardly assuaged when Carlsen, saying that he would show him his sleeping-and-living quarters, escorted him down the pitching, heaving corridor, as slippery and dark as a coal chute, to the gloom and wet cold of the radio cabin. Once there, Carlsen cleared away the litter of beer bottles and fragments of poundcake and helped Dancy pad out and rig up sleeping accommodations similar to his and roughly alongside them, between the floor and the edge of the settee. A number of blankets were available, and both men, soaked through, wrapped themselves up as thoroughly as they could. Carlsen then announced his intention of going to sleep. "Good night, Mr. Dancy," he added politely. During the whole time the two men spent together on the ship, Carlsen never addressed him without the formal prefix. The mate respectfully addressed him as "Captain" or "Mr. Carlsen."

Dancy did not get much sleep that first night; he lay for a long time in the cold, clammy cabin listening to and trying to identify the noises that incessantly echoed about the broken ship. "When a sea hit her beam-on, the whole ship would shudder from bow to stern," he later wrote in a magazine article. "A dozen and one bits of gear that had broken loose clattered and scraped against the decks and bulkheads. Persistently there was a pounding noise from the stern. It came again and again, at intervals of half a minute or so. That [must have been] the rudder being jarred back and forth by the heavy seas breaking under the stern. Carlsen, on the settee beside me, seemed to be quite composed and able to sleep through it all." Eventually, Dancy himself got in a couple of short periods of sleep. When he awoke in the morning, he found Carlsen up and about. "Would you like a cup of tea?" Carlsen asked, and Dancy looked on in fascination as the captain took a single lighted candle—the last of his original supply—in one hand and a tin of water in the other, and slowly brought the water to a boil.

At nine o'clock that morning, in seas that had moderated during the night, the Turmoil moved in for a further try—this time, by prearrangement between Carlsen and Captain Parker, at the bow of the Flying Enterprise, rather than at her stern. Before long, Dancy and Carlsen had the heaving line in and the first of the messenger lines looped around the bitts. Eventually, a one-inch Manila messenger made its appearance, followed by the steel tow-line itself. But this time the cable was not pulled back to the tug; the idea was to lead it through a chock in the bow and make a self-tightening noose around the bitts by cinching the cable together with a heavy shackle, which the Turmoil had already sent up, attached to the strongest messenger line. A shackle of this type is a hundred-pound U-shaped piece of steel with a removable cotter pin across its open end, and locking it into place was the most arduous and hazardous part of the operation for Carlsen and Dancy. It was a job that would have called for heavy labor by six or eight men even under relatively favorable circumstances, and when done by only two men, on a deck listing at sixty-five degrees and constantly rolling and pitching, it called for almost superhuman effort. It was also an exceedingly dangerous task, because at any moment the towline might have broken loose and whipped violently around the bitts, in all probability cutting the men to pieces. But after a bout of furious work they finished the job. Ten minutes later, looking down from the starboard rail toward the low side of the ship, they had the satisfaction of seeing the sea slipping steadily past them. At last the Flying

Enterprise was in tow—toward Falmouth, three hundred miles away.

As soon as the ships were safely under way, Carlsen scrambled amidships to check with the Turmoil by radio. When he emerged on deck again, he was carrying a one-pound tin of butter, which he had found in one of the ship's storerooms and which, in place of the heavy grease that lay stored in an inaccessible part of the ship, he applied to the towline at the bow chock to keep it from chafing and fraying. (On the following day, a sufficient quantity of regular grease, along with hot food and other badly needed supplies, was delivered to the men by line from the destroyer Willard Keith, which had relieved the Weeks an hour or so before the towline was secured.) Next, Carlsen suggested to Dancy that they make an excursion together to the ship's slop chest on the main deck to obtain dry clothes, and Dancy, in spite of the feeling of suffocation that the interior of the ship tended to inflict on him, went along. Because of the angle of the ship and the position of the locker, it was hard work getting the heavy steel door of the slop chest unlocked and open (Carlsen had been unable to do it by himself), but the two men managed it—by Dancy's lying on the vertically sloping deck with his feet braced against a bulkhead and Carlsen's climbing on his shoulders. Carlsen crawled into the room and handed out the dry clothing they needed, along with a few other supplies. When that was done, he took a pencil and notebook from his pocket and, as Dancy looked on in wonder, carefully noted down each article removed. That done, he climbed out again, closed the door, carefully locked it, and pocketed the key.

The arrival of the Turmoil at the side of the Flying Enterprise, the many efforts to get a line over to the disabled ship, Dancy's dramatic leap, and the eventual securing of a towline—all these events made for big headlines in the newspapers in this country. The British press was in a state of high excitement, too. "SHE'S IN TOW! HEADING HERE," a headline in the London *Evening News* of January 5th read, and the Manchester *Guardian* ran an editorial saying that Carlsen's quiet courage recalled the sea tales of Joseph Conrad, with modern touches, such as the captain's skill as a radio "ham." The editorial added that Carlsen deserved a happy ending to his story. During the next few days, as the wind and sea moderated and the two ships proceeded toward port at a fairly steady rate of three knots, it looked very much as if the ending were indeed going to be happy, and the press here and in Britain prepared to make the most of it. Not content with reporting every scrap of news that could be gleaned from the daily bulletins issued by the Willard Keith ("Tow riding easily. Captain Carlsen and Mr. Dancy chafed hands yesterday heaving food-transfer line on board. Attempting Tulley rig today for transfer more substantial load. . . . They tried cream and sugar in hot vegetable soup yesterday, mistaking it for coffee but enjoying it anyway"), several newspapers, wire services, and broadcasting and newsreel companies hired seagoing tugs, at fees ranging upward from fifteen hundred dollars a day, or airplanes, from two thousand dollars a day, to obtain their own reports and photographs.

The Associated Press chartered not only a tug for its reporters and photographers but also a courier tug to carry exposed film back to Falmouth. As for chartered airplanes, so many of them appeared over the Flying Enterprise during one day that the British Ministry of Civil Aviation felt obliged to instruct them to observe a counter-clockwise circuit in flying above the ship. On January 7th, the Associated Press reported that the progress of the ship toward port had become "more of a triumphal procession than a rescue," going on to say:

Some 750 yards behind the Turmoil came the wallowing, lopsided hulk of the Enterprise, with its stubborn skipper waving happily at a small parade of planes and ships which passed to cheer him on. To the stern he had affixed a new flagstaff from which fluttered the Stars and Stripes. In addition to the destroyer Willard Keith, which was hovering close, the French tug Abeille was bringing up the rear, tagging along in case of emergency.

The A.P. also reported that Falmouth was enjoying a boom, owing to the influx of more than a hundred newspapermen and many other people to await Carlsen's arrival. According to a Falmouth dispatch to the New York *Times*, these people included Carlsen's parents, who had been brought there from Denmark "as guests of a London newspaper." The *Times* also reported that a number of agents "seeking book, magazine, radio, television, and film rights—and even comic-strip rights—to his story" were lying in wait for Carlsen.

But on January 8th, the progress of the "triumphal procession" faltered, and early the next day, about fifty-seven miles southwest of Falmouth, it came to a halt. On the morning of the eighth, the wind and sea rose considerably, and Carlsen and Dancy, watching the weather from the high side of the Flying Enterprise, began to suspect that a storm was advancing upon them. They were right. As the day progressed, it became more and more difficult for them to make the journey to the bow every two hours, as they had been doing since the tow started, to grease the towline, and late in the afternoon the weather turned so savage that Captain Parker was forced to heave to. For about three hours, the Flying Enterprise lay drifting and rolling heavily at the end of the Turmoil's towline. The tow got under way again after nightfall, in moderating seas. The Flying Enterprise was now riding lower in the water than ever, and the commander of the Willard Keith, reporting on his radio conference with Carlsen at eight o'clock that night, noted that the captain "seemed a little concerned for the first time." But Dancy wrote later that Carlsen reacted to the situation with his customary composure, and that before going to sleep that night he turned as usual to "The Law of Seamen" and read for a while by candlelight. (The Willard Keith had replenished the supply of candles three days earlier.)

Both men slept for only a short time before being awakened by a loud crash that seemed to come from just outside the radio cabin, on the low side of the ship. Carlsen and Dancy quickly got up, ducked under the bedsheet they had rigged up as a windbreak, and peered down the heaving deck to see what had happened. The port lifeboat had broken partly loose and was banging against the hull. This melancholy clanging and crashing continued for some time; eventually, the last ropes holding the lifeboat parted, and it drifted away. Carlsen crawled up to his cabin and sent a message to the Willard Keith requesting that the lifeboat be machine-gunned as a menace to navigation. Then he rejoined Dancy in the radio cabin to sleep, but at one-thirty in the morning they were awakened again, this time by an even more ominous noise—six short blasts from the Turmoil's siren, an agreed-upon emergency signal. The tow had parted.

By now, the seas were so heavy that neither Carlsen nor Dancy could reach the bow, and Carlsen, in a radio conversation with Captain Parker, agreed that it would be useless to attempt to secure a new tow before daylight. They also discussed the possibility of trying another technique—rarely used and extremely difficult—of establishing a tow: Carlsen would let down his anchor chain, and the Turmoil and the Abeille, with a heavy line stretched between them, would approach the ship as in a mine-laying operation and try to pick it up. If all went well, they would then tow the Flying Enterprise to port by her own anchor. Carlsen, however, decided against the attempt; he knew that he could not stop the anchor chain from paying out once it had started, and if the operation was not a success, the anchor would only drag the ship still farther down at the head.

When daylight came, the weather was still heavy, and it was only with great difficulty that Carlsen and Dancy were able to get to the bow. At ten o'clock, the commander of the Willard Keith reported:

Turmoil skillfully maintaining the stern close off bow of Enterprise while Carlsen and Dancy work frantically with a hacksaw to cut off main shackle damaged during the night. Enterprise rolling to 80 degrees port and pitching, with spray breaking over the main bow. Turmoil awaiting wave of life jacket from Carlsen, which is "ready signal" to approach bow for passing line and new shackle.

But there was to be no ready signal. At about the time this message was being transmitted from the Willard Keith, a wave considerably bigger than the thirty-foot swells in which the ship had been riding struck the bow of the Flying Enterprise, knocked Carlsen off his feet and down the sloping deck, and actually washed him overboard for several feet. But he swam back, grasped one of the foremast shrouds, and managed to struggle up onto the deck. However, he was exhausted by the effort, and since Dancy had been half stunned by the impact of the wave and had nearly been washed overboard himself, the two men hauled themselves back to the radio cabin to rest and to wait for some improvement in the weather. Instead of improving, the weather worsened, and by three o'clock in the afternoon the skipper of the Willard Keith reported that it was impossible to pass a line in the existing seas. He added that the outlook for the immediate future was "not favorable." As the increasingly serious plight of the ship became known to the press, more and more chartered airplanes arrived on the scene, and circled around the Flying Enterprise until darkness set in.

By dawn the next day, January 10th, the wind had risen to a strong gale, and the prospects of getting a towline aboard began to appear depressingly remote to Carlsen and Dancy. "We can but hope and pray, hope and pray," Captain Parker told Carlsen during the eight-o'clock radio conference. In another radio contact, the captain of the Willard Keith relayed an offer from the Royal Air Force to pick up the two men by helicopter, but Carlsen declined it with thanks. He and Dancy spent most of the morning huddled in blankets in the radio cabin, with Carlsen doggedly reading on in "The Law of Seamen." Toward noon, the list of the ship increased, and it became obvious that the radio cabin was growing hourly more unsafe. Dancy went down to the cabin deck to inspect conditions on the low side of the ship and found water pouring through the cabin ports and weather doors. He attempted to tighten the bolts around several of the portholes, but failed to slow the inrush of water significantly. He returned to the radio cabin. When the seas began reaching into their only exit from the cabin, Carlsen and Dancy plainly saw that the time had come for them to move on. With great difficulty, they climbed up to the captain's cabin. The ship was now listing so heavily that the chintz curtains hanging at the portholes made a narrow angle with the ceiling.

Carlsen decided that they had better make provisions for a quick flight from the cabin. Fastening a strong rope to the starboard rail of the ship, he dropped it through the cabin's open door, which was now almost horizontal. Then they sat—or, rather, lay down— in two easy chairs resting against the lower wall of the cabin. The pounding of the seas against the hull, and the lurching of the whole ship, became more marked than ever. The men stayed where they were, saying very little. As time went on, they could observe the relentlessly narrowing angle between the chintz curtains and the ceiling. Underneath the door on the low side of the cabin, which was now like a trapdoor to a cellar, they could hear the seas sloshing about only a few feet below them in the interior of the ship. Waves were breaking over the bridge, and their spray poured in on the men from the open door overhead.

At about two o'clock, Dancy pulled himself up the rope, hand over hand, and took a look around outside. "She's almost on her beam-ends, Captain," he called down to Carlsen. Clambering up the rope, Carlsen joined him, to see for himself. After a long study, he finally said, "It's no good. She won't last." He lowered himself into the cabin

again to get Captain Parker on the radio and give his assent
to being picked up by helicopter. Then he rejoined Dancy,
and the two of them climbed over the deck rail and sat
smoking cigarettes on the side of the ship itself. A little
later, there was a loud explosion. The combined pressure
of water and air had blown out the door of the wheelhouse.

What happened after that is recorded in messages
emanating from the ships standing by:

3:08 P.M.—Keith: "Flying Enterprise is going
down."

3:09—Turmoil: "We have just received word that
the weather is too bad for the helicopter. She can't make it
and is returning to base. It is up to us to take them off
now."

3:16—Keith: "Flying Enterprise listing 80 degrees. Still afloat. Captain Carlsen and Dancy on starboard
of deck."

3:20—Keith: "Flying Enterprise now taking water
down stack."

3:22—Turmoil: "Dancy and Carlsen are preparing
to jump from the funnel. Stand by."

3:26—Keith: "Carlsen and Dancy have jumped
from the funnel."

3:32—Turmoil: "We have got both off Enterprise."

3:33—Keith: "Congratulations."

3:38—Turmoil: "Both men are O.K. and are now
in the captain's cabin changing their clothes."

3:44—Turmoil: "Flying Enterprise completely
covered in water. Cargo floating everywhere."

4:01—Turmoil: "Starboard bow just showing
above the waves. She is very brave. Keeps going down and
coming up."

4:03—Keith: "Enterprise now about 90 per cent
under water."

4:13—Keith: "In raging sea filled with debris, bow of Flying Enterprise rose 15 feet and slipped under at 1612 Z [4:12 P.M. Greenwich Mean Time] at Lat. 49-38N., Long. 04-23W."

The Turmoil did not linger at the scene, and Carlsen did not see the end of his ship. After he had changed into dry clothes and sipped some hot tea and rum in Captain Parker's cabin, he went up on the deck of the tug and took a last look at the Flying Enterprise as she lay sinking. Then he turned away. How the sight affected him is something that he has been reluctant to talk about. But some time later, in a letter to a Danish shipowner who had offered him a command in the Danish Merchant Marine, Carlsen, after turning the offer down, touched briefly on his attitude toward the Flying Enterprise. "I can say that I brought that ship up to perfection," he wrote. "Her engines and auxiliaries were purring comfortably as a cat, and I had the full loyalty of my crew, most of whom I had with me for a number of years." Then he added, "There was not as much as a piece of toast wasted." If Carlsen, who was capable of taking time to make an accounting of every dry sock he withdrew from the store of a half-capsized, disabled, and deserted vessel rolling and yawing in a tormented sea, could feel strongly about seeing a piece of toast wasted, how he felt at seeing his whole ship wasted is not easy to calculate.

With his companion, Carlsen, freshly shaved and wearing borrowed clothes and an old beret, stepped ashore in Falmouth on January 11th to a hero's welcome that was rendered all the warmer by public sympathy for his hard luck. There were cheering crowds, bursts of light from photographers' flash bulbs, laudatory civic speeches, and a big press conference—the first of a number of such receptions that Carlsen had to face in the coming weeks. At the press conference, Carlsen recounted his adventures with a modesty and earnestness that impressed his listeners, and he expressed his gratitude to all those who had taken part in the rescue and towing operations, and especially to Dancy and Captain Parker. Asked why he had decided to remain aboard his ship after everyone else had left, he replied, "I felt it was my duty to my owners." He firmly denied the rumor that he had stayed with the Flying Enterprise in order to collect some sort of salvage award for himself. "It is absolutely not true," he said. "The master of a ship cannot in any circumstances claim salvage. The thought of commercial or financial advantage has never entered into my mind at all."

Fending off entreaties for interviews from agents and promoters armed with contracts for magazine and motion-picture rights to his story, for personal appearances on television, and for his endorsement of all sorts of commercial products, Carlsen retired to a small hotel near Falmouth to spend some time alone with his parents, to telephone his wife and children back in Woodbridge, and to make plans for returning to his small home there as quietly as possible. But there was no way of escaping the clamor. Three days later, when he arrived in London by train, crowds broke through police lines at the station to press greetings and congratulations upon him. While he was in London, the Danish Ambassador to Great Britain, acting on behalf of King Frederik IX of Denmark, presented him with the Cross of the Order of the Dannebrog, one of Denmark's highest civilian orders; he was escorted to Lloyd's, where the Lutine bell (a ship's bell recovered from the British frigate Lutine, which, in 1799, sank, like the Flying Enterprise, off the English coast in an Atlantic gale) was tolled twice in his honor; and he was decorated before two thousand assembled insurance and underwriting people with Lloyd's rarely awarded Silver Medal, "in recognition of his outstanding courage and devotion to duty, by which he worthily upheld the high traditions of the sea." Then he flew back to the United States.

Before he got home to Woodbridge, the City of New York gave him a big, noisy harbor welcome, in which between three hundred and four hundred craft participated, and a ticker-tape parade up Broadway to City Hall, where Mayor Impellitteri presented him with the city's Medal of Honor. "I want you to know that you have enkindled in all of us a renewed faith in the all-pervading strength and dignity of man," the Mayor said—a sentiment that the press, without exception, expanded upon in editorials. "New York has its eyes on only one man today," an editorial in the *Times* read. "Captain Carlsen lost every battle with the hungry sea but the last. . . . He offered the world an example of stubborn courage, of steadfast loyalty to his responsibilities, of devotion to the traditions of his calling that inspired millions to exclaim to themselves, 'There is a man!'"

Amid all the public displays of enthusiasm, Carlsen maintained an appearance of somewhat puzzled calm, and the *Times* quoted him as having said to the Mayor, during his official reception downtown, "Frankly, I don't think I am entitled to this. I failed to bring my ship back into port." Such protestations only heightened the general admiration for his modesty and increased the general desire to reward him. The Senate voted unanimously to direct

the Maritime Administration to give him the Merchant
Marine Distinguished Service Medal. The French government informed him that it was giving him the Ordre du
Mérite Maritime, and the Belgian government gave him a
similar decoration. State and provincial governments and
the mayors of municipalities throughout the world sent
greetings to him and urged him to accept in person, at the
earliest convenient time, medals of honor and keys to cities.
The city of Gloucester, Massachusetts, wanted to give him
its Mariner's Award, and the American Bureau of Shipping
informed him that it was decorating him with its Medal of
Valor. Altogether, Carlsen was presented with thirty-three
medals. The findings of a United States Coast Guard
inquiry into the sinking of the Flying Enterprise called
Carlsen's epic "certainly an act beyond the call of duty, and
an outstanding example of the best traditions of the sea"—
though it did add, mildly, that if Carlsen had accepted the
services of some of the crewmen who volunteered to stay
aboard with him and wait for a tow, "the outcome might
well have been different."

There were other tokens of appreciation. At home
in Woodbridge, Carlsen found great piles of congratulatory
cables and letters from private individuals throughout the
world, and an even greater volume of similar messages was
arriving every day at Isbrandtsen headquarters, on lower
Broadway. "It was just amazing," an Isbrandtsen man
who was assigned the task of coping with some of the public
uproar said, a while later. "One morning, I came into my
office and found nine sacks of mail for Carlsen by my desk.
People from here to Timbuctoo sent in admiring letters.
We had women baking cakes and knitting socks by the
dozen and mailing them in here for Carlsen. The cakes were

the worst nuisance, because they would arrive broken in the mailbags and the sticky crumbs would get all over the other mail as it spilled out. Letters, cakes, songs, poems— everything. All in all, he must have received about twelve thousand letters of congratulation."

Along with these letters, Carlsen found awaiting him, in large numbers, further financial offers for exclusive literary, motion-picture, and television rights to his story, and these, together with requests for his endorsement of commercial products, amounted, according to an Isbrandtsen man, to something like two hundred and fifty thousand dollars. One motion-picture company proposed a minimum guarantee of a hundred and fifty thousand dollars for a picture based on his experiences. A Canadian beer company offered him a tour of Canada on behalf of a brand of beer; the brewer was waiting at a New York hotel with a check for thirty thousand dollars as an advance. And the owner of a knitting mill wanted Carlsen to testify that on the Flying Enterprise he had kept warm in a sweater turned out by the mill.

Then, there were offers of jobs. One man offered Carlsen a distributorship in a big soft-drink company; another offered him the management of a pleasure-cruiser establishment with dock facilities in Florida. And there were invitations to him and his family to spend free vacations at various resorts in Florida, Pennsylvania, and California. Carlsen turned everybody and everything down. He frequently said, "I don't want a seaman's honest attempt to save his ship used for any commercial purpose. I don't want to get anything out of it." All he wanted, he made plain to everyone, was to get back to sea. Isbrandtsen, who had promised him command of another ship, gave him one as soon as a replacement for the Flying Enterprise could be bought from the government. The new ship, a C-2 cargo carrier, forty feet longer than her predecessor but of about the same vintage, was rechristened the Flying Enterprise II, and, with Carlsen on the bridge, she sailed from Mobile, Alabama, late in April, 1952, for Le Havre.

From then until this book was written, Carlsen and the Flying Enterprise II have been assigned to the round-the-world service of the Isbrandtsen Company (which since 1962 has been merged into a new company, American Export-Isbrandtsen Lines). There are ten ships in this round-the-world service. Each ship has its own route; Carlsen's covers a 25,000-mile circuit that begins at New York and generally includes calls at Beirut, Alexandria, Port Said, Bombay, Singapore, Hong Kong, Kobe, Nagoya, Yokohama, San Francisco, and a number of West and East Coast ports before ending in New York five months later. The elapsed time between the end of one of these voyages and the start of another is usually from three to five days.

During one of these layovers, about six and a half years after Carlsen's ordeal aboard the Flying Enterprise, a friend of Carlsen's who worked for Isbrandtsen arranged for me to spend part of an afternoon with the captain on board the Flying Enterprise II, at the company's pier in Gowanus Bay. "It's not often nowadays that Kurt has a visit from anybody connected with the press," the Isbrandtsen man said. "Things have been pretty quiet for him these past few years, and I know he's glad to have the notoriety behind him. He just keeps going around the world—around and around and around. He's a little heavier now than he used to be, and he's taken to smoking cigars instead of cigarettes, but he still goes in strong for amateur radio, and he's built himself a dandy personal one-kilowatt transmitter to replace the one he lost when the old Enterprise went down. A good skipper, well liked by passengers and crew. They say he relaxes quite a bit with people when he's at sea."

It was raining when I arrived at the Isbrandtsen pier, and the unloading of cargo from Carlsen's ship was going on under huge conical arrangements of tarpaulins that covered the open hatches and towered above the decks like a row of great dingy wigwams. The Flying Enterprise II is a good-sized freighter, and she was painted in the manner of all Isbrandtsen ships—dark-gray hull, with the name "ISBRANDTSEN" all along her side in six-foot-high letters; white housing amidships; and light-buff masts and funnel. I could see that the ship had seen a good deal of service; along the waterline the plates of her hull were dented so deeply in places it was possible to detect the outlines of the vessel's unyielding ribs.

I found Carlsen at his desk in the captain's cabin, where he was working on the ship's accounts and tapping away at the keyboard of a small electric calculating machine. He had very much the same stocky, square-jawed, earnest look that I had seen in newspaper photographs of him after the sinking of his ship. He had taken off the jacket of his blue suit and was in shirtsleeves. Attached to his belt was a little plastic holster with a ball-point pen clipped into it. Greeting me with quiet affability, he asked me to take a seat and wait a few moments while he finished up his computations.

I sat down on a couch, upholstered in flowered

chintz, that stood under a water color entitled "An Eastern Mosque." The portholes, whose brass fixtures were immaculately polished, were decorated with curtains of a matching flowered chintz, and the cabin furniture also included a curtained bookcase; a polished sideboard covered with olive-green cloth, on which rested two small silver-colored pots of philodendrons, whose tendrils radiated outward across the cloth and trailed around its edges in regimented symmetry; a mess table covered with the same kind of olive-green material, fringed with heavy tassels; an electric fan; a comfortable armchair and a hassock of vaguely Moorish design; and a filing cabinet. A colored print of a square-rigger hung on the wall above Carlsen's desk, a print showing a clock tower hung near the mess table, and an oil painting depicting the Flying Enterprise under tow in stormy seas hung over the sideboard and the trailing philodendron leaves.

Carlsen finished his calculations and turned to me. "We don't have a purser on this ship, so I take on the paperwork," he said, adding, with a certain vehemence, "I'm a pen-pusher." He got up and went over to put some papers away in the filing cabinet, and as he did so I noticed that he walked with a pronounced limp. I asked him what had happened, and he told me that he had injured his foot in a fall from the wheelhouse to the deck during a severe Atlantic storm nearly a year ago; he had had the foot X-rayed in San Francisco a few months later, he said, and found that his left ankle and heel were fractured. "My first injury at sea in thirty years," he said. There was a long pause, which I broke by asking him to tell me something of the voyage he had just completed. "Oh, apart from that Atlantic storm, I guess it was pretty average," Carlsen said. "We brought in a sealed cargo from Bombay, though—five hundred tons of old silver currency that the Indian government was sending over here to be melted down and used as credit. Now that India has its own currency, I guess they don't want those kings on their coins any more. The stuff was unloaded here yesterday and taken off in armored cars to the Treasury for assay."

I told Carlsen that I had really come to talk to him about his efforts to bring the Flying Enterprise into port seven years ago, and he did not seem particularly pleased at the idea. "I don't know why my trouble with the Enterprise should hold any interest for anybody after all this time," he said, cocking his head a little to one side in a set, dogged way. "Anyway, all that business about staying on the ship—it's become almost a joke with some people. I don't care for it." After a while, however, he seemed to conclude that my interest was not frivolous, and began to respond to questions about his thirteen days on the listing ship, elucidating—and even illustrating for me with pencilled diagrams—various technical matters, and adding little personal details, such as how, one morning when he woke up, he felt such a need to get rid of the grime and grease on his skin that he washed his face and hands with foam from one of the ship's fire extinguishers, and how the lack of hot food and the chafing of his hands from hauling on lines bothered him far less than the soreness of his feet and ankles, brought on by the twisting and warping effect of constantly having to scramble in the V-shaped troughs between the listing decks and the bulkheads. "My shoes were in very sad shape afterward," he told me, shaking his head slightly. "When I got to England, I had to throw them away."

Carlsen was noticeably less talkative about matters that did not touch on the purely physical side of his experience, and when he did speak of them, he gave me the impression of a man who, with time, has recast some of his memories in a new mold. For instance, when I asked him, rather casually, whether he had not felt very lonely on the deserted ship, he said, in a suddenly resentful voice, "That's not true at all!" Mildly puzzled, I said that I was sure that in the files of the Isbrandtsen Company I had come across a message from him to his wife saying that he was well but lonesome. "Not true at all!" Carlsen said, in a strong voice. "Why should I send such a message? Why should I have been lonesome? A shipmaster is used to solitude. Hell, when I'm out in the Pacific I sometimes sit in my cabin for fourteen days at a stretch and never see a goddam soul! You can't sit down and yack away with officers and passengers all the time. You have to keep a certain distance when you're the master. You know the old saying—familiarity breeds contempt."

A bit later, I asked Carlsen how he had felt at seeing Dancy come aboard the ship. "Well, of course, it would make it easier for me to have someone aboard," he said slowly, as if in reply to a theoretical question. He added, after a few moments of silence, "If you mean how did I *feel* about it, I had no emotional feelings one way or another. I've had Dancy to my house for dinner since then. All very pleasant—we get along all right. He's first mate on a British tanker now. Dancy was a young British gentleman—very courteous, very correct. In six days on the Enterprise, it was always 'Mr. Dancy' and 'Mr. Carlsen' to each other, you know. That's the way it was. Whether the ship was eighty degrees on her side or not, I was still the master, and he was smart enough to recognize it."

I observed that I had read an article by Dancy in which he spoke repeatedly of being oppressed by a strong fear of being helplessly confined in the interior of the ship, and I asked Carlsen if Dancy had said anything to him about this fear.

"Oh, yes, he told me he had claustrophobia," Carlsen said.

"Even under ordinary conditions?" I asked.

"Oh, sure," Carlsen said.

"And he still went below the waterline to tighten bolts around the portholes?" I asked.

"Oh, yes, he went down there. I just told him to forget about his claustrophobia," Carlsen said.

There was a knock at the door of the cabin, and the chief mate entered with a large sheaf of papers.

"Sorry to interrupt, Captain," he said. "I thought I'd let you know that Mrs. Carlsen is here. She's finished her shopping, and she said she'd have some coffee in the dining room. She asked me to remind you about the doctor's appointment for that X-ray. She'll go along with you."

"O.K.," Carlsen said.

"And these reports here," the mate added, flourishing the papers in his hand. "Could you look them over, Captain?"

"Yes," Carlsen said, and he told me abruptly that I'd have to excuse him for twenty minutes or so.

Leaving the cabin, I went down to the dining room to see Mrs. Carlsen, whom I'd talked to on the telephone several times but had never met. She is a pleasant-looking woman, with a diffident manner, but I found her in a talkative mood. She told me she was worried about her husband's fractured foot, which she was not sure had healed properly, and said she had persuaded him to have it X-rayed again. "He's always taking on so much and working so hard," she said. "Some people just seem to burden themselves with responsibilities. Kurt is like that. When he started going to sea for this company, in 1943, he was a second officer, and I thought, Well, when he gets to be first officer, things will be different and he'll have more free time. But he didn't. When he became first officer, he took on more work, and I thought, Well, when he's captain, it will be different, and now I find he takes on more than ever. All that paperwork, as well as running the ship. He never complains about the pressure; he just seems to hold it all in. And when it gets too much, then he gets very quiet; he just pushes everybody away, and you can't talk to him.

"If you ask me, he had a great hurt, losing his ship like that. He always has had such a powerful sense of his duty. I remembered that when I first heard the ship was in trouble and he was staying aboard, I was so afraid for what might happen. And those newspapermen were driving me crazy, telephoning me at home at all hours. Asking all kinds of crazy questions. Do the children love their father? How is the dog taking it? I said, 'For heaven's sake, why do you ask me that when my husband is sitting out there on the sea?' And then they put it on the television that my husband had said he'd bring in his ship or go down with her, and although I soon found out that he really hadn't said he would go down with her, I was afraid for a while that something in his mind might have slipped—that he really meant to do that. Oh, I prayed for him. The pastor was with me, you know. At home, we don't talk about Kurt's experiences. Now this ship keeps him busier than ever. He has very little time off between trips, and even while the ship is in, he's usually working aboard her all day. He never really gets a chance to get into family life, never sees the children growing up. Sometimes, when the ship's in, he'll come home so tired that he'll just lie down on the couch before dinner and go right to sleep."

When I returned to Carlsen's cabin, he was still talking to the mate, so I occupied myself by strolling around the room. As the mate left, I was looking at the colored print of the clock tower; I now noticed that it had a water stain across it. "Doesn't look bad for having spent eighteen months forty-two fathoms down on the bottom of the Atlantic, does it?" Carlsen called out to me from his swivel chair. Smiling wryly at my surprise, he told me that the print had once hung in his cabin on the Flying Enterprise. It was recovered from the wreck in 1953, along with some cargo and mail, by a team of Italian salvors, he said; the salvors had sent it to him as a souvenir.

"It was a strange business, that salvage operation," he went on. "After the Enterprise went down, there were all sorts of rumors that the ship had been carrying bullion, or some special cargo—the Russians were even saying that she was loaded with V-2 parts from Germany. As far as I or my owners knew, there was nothing in the cargo that wasn't shown on the ship's manifest. We were all amazed when the newspapers printed stories about how these Italian salvors had recovered a quarter of a million dollars in United States and British currency from her. We didn't believe the stories until we found that the money came from the mailbags in the holds. It had been sent by Swiss

banks to New York banks by registered mail as part of
their regular transactions."

I asked Carlsen whether, aboard his present ship,
he had ever passed over the spot where the Flying Enterprise lay.

"Yes, I have," Carlsen said.

"How did you feel about that?" I asked.

"How do you think I felt?" he said harshly. He
paused for a considerable time, and then said, in a very
quiet voice, "You don't realize what a thing like that means
to a shipmaster. The Enterprise was my *home*. When I was
standing on her deck, I could feel her through my feet. I
could stand there on the bridge and I could feel her re-
sponding to my wish. I could feel when she was in trouble.
And when that storm hit her and I had to order everybody
off, I felt, somehow, that I could still bring her into port.
Don't ask any more questions about those thirteen days.
Thirteen days and thirteen nights on a dead ship. A dead
ship is not like a live ship. You just don't know what it
means. I can't really describe those days and nights. They're
mine, they always will be mine, and I don't see that they
would be of any interest to anybody else. How could I
leave her? How could I leave her and stand off on a goddam tug?" Carlsen's voice rose again, taking on an indignant tone. "Suppose I'd left her and someone had managed
to get aboard her—the way a British trawler crew got
aboard the American Farmer, years ago, after her captain
had abandoned her as a derelict—and found that she wasn't
sinking after all! Suppose I had abandoned the Enterprise
and she didn't sink! Can you think of anything more de-
grading?"

Carlsen paused again, and from outside the cabin

I could hear the rumbling of winches and the hoarse shouts of longshoremen. Then, not looking at me, and with his head cocked to one side in a set way, he went on, "It isn't a very glorious thing to lose your ship. These people, these promoters, thought I would want to take money for what I did. Well, why should I have accepted something that was so morally wrong? It would be extremely against my principles to go and do a thing like that. In my life, every goddam day I see people they don't want to do even what they're supposed to do." Carlsen made a gesture toward the accounts on his desk. "Some of these fellows we've got here on the docks—some of them will get thirty or forty dollars a day just for being there. You don't get people to put in the work any more.

"Here!" He yanked open a drawer of his desk, and took out a big steel bolt and a typewritten sheet of paper. He angrily held them up in front of me. "Look!" he said. "Here's a report on the performance of a crewman I got here this morning. You know what it says under 'Mechanical Ability'? 'Good,' it says. Just look at that work! Mechanical ability!" Carlsen tossed the bolt contemptuously on the desk. "Good! Huh! Now do you understand why I told everybody, volunteers and all, to get the hell off my little Enterprise when she heeled over on her side? Who is there to trust?"

Something Wrong With The Island

When the British liner Stirling Castle steamed into Southampton Harbor from Cape Town on the morning of November 3, 1961, she was met by a cutter carrying a large contingent of reporters, photographers, and radio and television crews, who scrambled aboard eager to seek out the most unassuming lot of celebrities that any of them had probably ever encountered—two hundred and sixty-two men, women, and children constituting the entire native population of Tristan da Cunha, a tiny island in the remote waters of the South Atlantic. The islanders were humbly dressed—the men in well-worn, rumpled suits and cloth caps, and the women, for the most part, in shawls or cheap bandannas, with old-fashioned full, long dresses. Their faces were somewhat big-boned, and their manner markedly shy. Their complexions ranged from light to swarthy, indicating a variety of ethnic backgrounds, but their common language was English, spoken in archaic accents somewhat reminiscent of the speech of coachmen and domestics in the novels of Charles Dickens. They were, in fact, all interrelated, having among them only seven family names—Glass, Swain, Green, Rogers, Repetto, Lavarello, and Hagan.

Newspaper dispatches from Cape Town had already informed the public that the way of life the strangers were accustomed to in their island home was as plain as their appearance and as anachronistic as their speech. Descendants, mainly, of shipwrecked mariners, they had inherited and contentedly perpetuated a spare, castaways' civilization based on such elemental activities as raising potatoes, which they hauled home in bullock carts mounted on solid wooden wheels; fishing from canvas-hulled longboats; and carding wool sheared from island-grown sheep and converting it into yarn on spinning wheels. In recent years, Great Britain, which annexed Tristan da Cunha in the early part of the nineteenth century, had been making sporadic efforts to superimpose some aspects of its own civilization on that of the islanders, but in the press of other matters it was easy to forget about them, tucked away as they were in geographical obscurity, seventeen hundred miles west of Cape Town, twenty-one hundred miles east of Rio de Janeiro, and fifteen hundred miles south of their nearest neighbors, on the island of St. Helena. Until the people of Tristan left their island, it was known as one of the most isolated inhabited spots in the world—and, except in the eyes of its natives, not a very inviting spot at that.

Tristan da Cunha—the largest of three islands that, ranged within a radius of twenty miles, are collectively designated by the same name—presents a formidable face to the sea. A cone-shaped mass, sixty-seven hundred feet high, with the crater of an extinct volcano in its cloud-ringed peak, it rests on a base, about eight miles in diameter, that is bounded by a bleak wall of cliffs of blackish lava rising almost unbroken to a height of between eight hundred and two thousand feet, either directly from the water or, in a few places, from narrow strips of rock-strewn but relatively level ground. These strips constitute Tristan's only arable land, and prior to the departure of its population one of them—a meagre plateau, four and a half miles long and half a mile wide, on the northwest coast—was the site of the island's only settlement, formally designated as Edinburgh but ordinarily known just as "the settlement."

Wanderers in search of the exotic have not been lured to Tristan as they have been to the South Pacific, for while the island enjoys a climate that might be called mild, in the sense that the temperature has never been known to drop below thirty-eight degrees or to rise above seventy-eight, the place is subject to terrible gales, torrential rains, and raging seas. In recent times, navigators have tended to bypass Tristan, not only because it has no harbor and its offshore waters are notoriously treacherous but because vessels have had little reason for stopping there. At times during this century, eighteen months have elapsed without a single vessel's casting anchor off the island's coast.

A hundred years ago, though, the situation was somewhat different. Numerous merchant ships under sail, taking advantage of the trade winds that carried them past Tristan, and numerous New England whaling vessels working the South Atlantic had no alternative but to stop at the settlement's anchorage in order to replenish their dwindling reserves of fresh water and other supplies. Many other ships stopped at the island most unwillingly, driven by storms against its rocky shores, and for these Tristan became the final port of call. Their crews—and those of vessels that foundered off Nightingale and Inaccessible, Tristan's two satellite islands—made their way, if they were lucky, to the settlement. Most of the castaways simply waited there for another ship to come along and take them home, but a few decided to go no farther and became islanders themselves.

The people of Tristan, as much of the world was aware by the time they had reached Southhampton, did not abandon their island gladly. They were obliged to flee it because of the same volcanic forces that originally created it, and which, after a preliminary series of earth tremors, struck again—not, of course, through Tristan's extinct crater but through the ground right on the edge of the settlement, where there rose a great bubble of earth that presently burst and became a volcano itself. Under the direction of a resident British administrator, the islanders hastily put out to sea in their longboats, and were picked up by commercial fishing vessels, which then put them aboard a Dutch liner. The liner took them to Cape Town, where they were transferred to the Stirling Castle, bound for England.

At the end of the voyage, they looked subdued and bewildered as they stood around on deck with the flickering of flash bulbs playing over them like heat lightning. Briefly but politely, and with dignity, they replied to the questions of the reporters, recalling, in their curious accents, details of the "wolcano on our hisland." They seemed pretty much agreed that it was very strange to venture into "the houtside warld" but that, considering the circumstances, they were "werry 'appy" to take refuge in England. Among various English officials on hand to deliver welcoming speeches was a representative of the Colonial Office, which had arranged for the islanders to be housed at Pendell Camp, an unoccupied British Army barracks in Surrey, until it could be determined whether they might safely return to Tristan or, if not, where they could best be settled permanently in Britain. The islanders took the formalities fairly well in stride, courteously giving each speaker generous applause, but they seemed altogether confused when the man from the Colonial Office, having uttered his first sentence of welcome, perceived that the television cameramen weren't quite ready for him and, after a pause, began his speech all over again. It was like one century gazing at another.

At last, the speechmaking ended, and the islanders were escorted ashore and driven in chartered buses (instead of bullock carts), over paved roads (instead of dirt ruts), past automobiles and motorcycles (instead of donkeys), to Pendell Camp. Not surprisingly, by the time they arrived there many of them, especially the older people, were numb with exhaustion from the experiences they had undergone since their flight from Tristan, twenty-five days earlier. But there were exceptions, among them one of the Glasses, a young man who was found by a London *Times* reporter seated in the camp's social center, in his cloth cap and scarf, studying an article in a slick-paper magazine entitled "How to Change Your Personality."

Tristan da Cunha, together with its satellite islands, was discovered in 1506—some three hundred years before the first settlers arrived—by a Portuguese expedition under the command of Admiral Tristão da Cunha. The Admiral apparently did not land anyone on Tristan, but in 1643 a party from a Dutch ship went ashore there and took on fresh water, with which the island is abundantly supplied by streams flowing down from a lake in the crater at its peak. Later in the seventeenth century, other ships, representing either the Dutch United East India Company or its English counterpart, visited all three islands to explore the feasibility of using them as revictualling stations for merchant shipping on the great southern trade route from Europe to India via Cape Horn, but the masters of the vessels, after looking around, concluded that Nightingale and Inaccessible were uninhabitable, and therefore out of the question, and that the usefulness of Tristan was dubious at best, since it had no harbor. The two companies thereupon abandoned any notions they may have had of colonizing the group.

As it happened, the island was first settled under the leadership of an American. He was Jonathan Lambert, of Salem, Massachusetts, who in 1810, at the age of thirty-eight, engaged the captain of the Boston ship Baltic to land him on Tristan, with two companions, one of whom was a native of Italy now remembered as Thomas Currie but whose name originally was probably Tomaso Corri, and the other a man named Williams. Lambert's idea, too, was to establish a revictualling station, and, less cautious than his predecessors, he went prepared to set himself right up in business, taking along geese, chickens, turkeys, ducks, pigs, potatoes, sugar cane, and corn, plus a coffee tree, with which to start a farm and raise the produce he expected to barter with passing ships.

In July of the following year, Lambert placed an advertisement in the Boston *Gazette* announcing that he was creating on Tristan "a Home where I can enjoy life without the embarrassments which have hitherto constantly attended me . . . and remain, if possible, far removed beyond the reach of chicanery and ordinary misfortune," and inviting ships to call there for supplies "at a reasonable price." It was a remarkable ad, for in it Lambert boldly proclaimed himself the sole proprietor of the whole island group, which he had renamed the Islands of Refreshment, and which, he declared, was thereafter to be regarded as a sovereign state, with a flag of its own.

Just how much business Lambert did on Tristan nobody knows, but his enjoyment of the island as a haven from misfortune lasted only a couple of years. In May, 1812, he, Williams, and another American, name unknown, who had joined the venture, were drowned in the course of an offshore fishing expedition. That left Currie as the only inhabitant of the island—a distinction he seems to have held for some time. He was not entirely without occasional company, though, since word had got around that Tristan was now a source of food as well as water. Some of his callers were quite unwelcome. During the War of 1812, a number of American privateers used the island group as a refuge from which to dart forth and attack British merchantmen, and Currie complained that some of the landing parties from the American ships, instead of buying or trading for what they wanted, simply made off with it. In 1815, or thereabouts, Currie was joined by two would-be settlers named John Tankard and John Talsen, but apparently they were soon discouraged, for they left within a few months. Meanwhile, the war had ended, but several of the privateers continued to hang about and prey on shipping near the islands—to "the great annoyance of all vessels" in the South Atlantic, according to the British

governor of the Cape of Good Hope. In 1816, in an effort
to rid the area of these marauders—and also as a precaution
against Tristan's being used as a base in any attempt to
rescue Napoleon from St. Helena—Britain took possession
of the islands, no other power ever having formally claimed
them. To make their claim stick and to accomplish their
military purpose, the British established a garrison of fifty
men, accompanied by a number of civilian workers, ten
women, and twelve children, on Tristan's northwest coast,
which the newcomers shared with Currie and a Spanish
youth known as Bastiano Pancho Comilla, whom Currie
had imported to help him with the farm work.

The garrison and its entourage were withdrawn
from Tristan after a year, during which Currie died and
Comilla departed, but the island was not left wholly unoccupied, for one of the soldiers (with the permission of his
commander), his wife and two children, and two of the
civilian workers stayed on. The settlers were William Glass,
a thirty-year-old corporal in the Royal Artillery, who was
born in Kelso, on the Scottish border; his wife, a colored
woman from the Cape, and the first two of sixteen children
she ultimately bore him; and John Nankivel and Samuel
Burnell, two stonemasons from Plymouth. Reviving Lambert's old dream of running a farm and trading station, the
three men formed a partnership based on a written agreement that all their possessions, at the time consisting mainly
of some grain and a few head of livestock, were to be com-
munally owned, and that in their relations with one another
none of them "shall assume any superiority whatever, but
all [are] to be considered as equal in every respect." In
time, however, Glass, more of a natural leader than the

others, came to be called "Governor," and for the rest of his life he was looked up to as the island's first citizen.

In 1820, there began a series of shipwrecks that were to provide the little community not only with a variety of much needed salvage, including tools and lumber (the only indigenous island growth approximating a tree is a shrub-like species of buckthorn), but with the additional inhabitants it needed to keep it going in the face of emigrations and a series of nautical misfortunes. In that year, the adult-male population was cut by a third when the partners, having killed a number of elephant seals, which in those days swarmed along Tristan's rocky coast, sent Burnell to the Cape of Good Hope to barter the animals' skins for various items and he failed to return. The island's permanent population inched up again when eight men from three separate wrecks arrived on the island. A few months later, the Blendon Hall, bound from London to Bombay, foundered off Inaccessible, eighteen miles southwest of Tristan. Fifty of the fifty-two persons on board survived, and managed to stick it out on Inaccessible for several months, living on sea birds and their eggs, while a flat-bottomed boat was built from the remains of the Blendon Hall. The boat proved seaworthy enough to take a few of them to Tristan, where Glass and his fellow-settlers received them in most hospitable fashion, giving up their beds to them and making a series of dangerous longboat trips to bring the rest of the survivors across. Two of them elected to remain on Tristan—an Englishman named Stephen White and a half-caste Portuguese servant girl called Peggy. The others were taken off the island in January, 1822, by two passing vessels. This left the adult-male population of Tristan at eleven, but within a year seven men quit the island, bringing the total down to four—two men named Alexander Cotton and Richard Riley, who were among the castaways who had arrived just after Burnell's departure, plus Glass and White—who, together with Mrs. Glass, Peggy (now Mrs. White), and six children, constituted the whole community.

This group was in no way enhanced by the next newcomer—a man named Smith, who had once been captain of a large ship but latterly had been reduced to running a small, ramshackle sealing sloop. Landing on Tristan quite insane, he roamed the island alone for several months, and was eventually found dead. A more welcome arrival was Augustus Earle, a young English artist, who became an involuntary sojourner under circumstances rather different from those of most of the stranded transients. In 1824, when a sloop on which he was a passenger called at Tristan to take on water and to barter for potatoes, Earle went ashore to make some sketches, and decided to stay overnight while the islanders were loading the supplies onto the vessel from their longboats. In the morning, just as a longboat crew was preparing to push off with the last load of potatoes, atop which sat Earle, a severe squall broke, making it impossible for the boat to reach the sloop. The squall soon became a gale of such violence that the sloop's master was obliged to seek the safety of deep water, and sailed away, leaving Earle stranded. The artist stayed eight months on Tristan, as a house guest of the Glasses, while waiting for another boat to pick him up, and it is clear from a journal he kept during that time that he was impressed with the starkness of the island:

Looking out from my abode, no spot in the world can be more desolate. . . . The roar of the sea is almost

deafening, and the wind rushing furiously down the per-
pendicular sides of the mountains, which are nearly nine
hundred feet high, and are masses of craggy rocks, has the
most extraordinary and almost supernatural effect.

Day after day, during his sojourn on Tristan, Earle
scrambled from one rocky vantage point to another, looking
out to sea for deliverance, and he soon reduced his clothes
to tatters, whereupon Glass considerately ran him up a new
pair of trousers, Robinson Crusoe style, with a sailcloth
front and a back made of dried goatskin, hairy side out.
Earle, for his part, made a sketch of Glass in which the
subject is shown in a tartan bonnet, a loose, smocklike shirt,
baggy pants, and a pair of moccasins, placidly smoking a
long churchwarden pipe as he leans on a rough wooden
fence (fashioned from the spars of wrecked vessels, the
artist explains in his journal), with a couple of hens scratch-
ing around in the earth nearby. In the background is a
low-slung thatch-roofed house that resembles the crofters'
cottages of the Hebrides, and, indeed, most of the twentieth-
century Tristan houses. "The houses, and all around them,
had an air of comfort, cleanliness, and plenty, truly English," Earle wrote. "The cows, oxen, sheep and poultry, all
thrive here; but the pigs, owing to their eating so much
kelp or seaweed, have a very fishy unpleasant taste."

A full year after Earle finally got a lift off the
island (he later was a draftsman aboard the Beagle on the
voyage that Charles Darwin made so famous), the sloop
that had left him there turned up again, this time with two
male passengers who went ashore intending to stay not
just overnight but for good. One of them, to be sure, soon
became disenchanted with the place and departed, but the
other, a fifty-two-year-old English bachelor named Thomas

Swain, had a good reason to stay on, and he did. Swain, after spending eighteen years in the British Navy and serving under Nelson in the Mediterranean during the French Revolutionary Wars, had deserted and been captured by the French, who compelled him to fight in their own Navy against Britain. While he had been thus engaged, he was captured by the British, who, since he shrewdly did not reveal his true identity, held him as a prisoner of war for the duration. With such a past, Swain found a hideaway like Tristan much to his liking, and he remained there until he died, in 1863.

All the Swains of Tristan are his descendants, and the fact that there are any such can be accounted for by a yearning for gentle companionship that in 1827 impelled the old Navy deserter and four other bachelors, newly arrived on the island, to commission a ship captain to import five women from St. Helena—at the rate, according to legend, of eight bushels of potatoes per passenger. The women—four mulattoes and a Negro—arrived in due course, with four children in tow. This influx, combined with other comings, and despite a few goings, brought the total population of Tristan up to twenty-four—seven men, six women, and eleven children. During the next eight years, the total rose to forty-two—a population explosion by any standards.

Although Britain's claim to Tristan was undisputed and the islanders always thought of themselves as British subjects, for decades the outside world exerted its greatest influence on them through the crews of American whalers. The Americans bartered flour, tea, coffee, tobacco, clothes, and tools for Tristan's fresh farm produce, and, with so many of their vessels scouring the nearby seas, they inevitably accounted for a relatively large proportion of both shipwrecks and new settlers. In 1835, for example, when Tristan's adult-male population was down to six, it was increased fifty per cent by one American shipwreck alone—that of the schooner Emily, out of New York. On reaching the settlement, three of the surviving members of the crew—William Daley, Peter Miller, and Peter Green—decided to stay there. All three were soon married—Daley to one of Glass's several daughters, Miller to a daughter of one of the women from St. Helena, and Green to another daughter of the same woman. All the Tristan Greens are his descendants. Not many months after the wreck of the Emily, another of Glass's daughters married a man named Rogers, who had arrived on Tristan as a member of the crew of an American whaler and remained behind when it sailed.

Rogers left the island after a while, never to return, but in the meantime he had sired offspring from whom all the Rogerses of Tristan are descended. Samuel Johnson, a crewman of another American whaler, who quit his ship to join the Tristan community and presently married Glass's eldest daughter, Mary, appears to have taken his domestic responsibilities more seriously, for when, in 1847, after spending fourteen years on the island, he moved back to the United States, he brought his wife and children with him. His family was the first of several to migrate from Tristan to this country in the middle of the century, with obviously disruptive effects on life in the little settlement, but at least Johnson's place as one of its able-bodied men was soon filled by Andrew Hagan, the captain of an American whaler, who married yet another Glass daughter, Selina, and became the progenitor of all the Tristan Hagans.

Although Tristan's population had tended to fluctuate sharply right from the start, the general drift during the first half of the nineteenth century was upward—a state of affairs that made it steadily more difficult for the islanders to support themselves, since, aside from what food they could obtain by fishing in the precarious surrounding waters, they were almost entirely dependent on what they could grow in the little fertile land at their disposal. This was probably the underlying reason that for half a dozen years, beginning around 1850, Tristaners chose to leave the island in ever-increasing numbers. For example, by the time Glass died—of cancer, in 1853, when he was sixty-seven—five of his fifteen children had left the island and were living in New England whaling ports. Three years after his death, his widow, three of her sons, five of her daughters, a son-in-law, and ten of her grandchildren decided to follow them and boarded a whaler bound for New Bedford. In fact, the year 1856 must have been an exceptionally discouraging one for those Tristan people who loved the island too much to leave it. A month after the departure of the Glass party, the British colonial authorities, having been informed that the remaining inhabitants were in serious want, sent a man-of-war to Tristan with an offer to evacuate them to the Cape of Good Hope and settle them there, and more than half of them—some forty-five, it appears—ultimately accepted. After they were gone, the population of the island stood at a mere twenty-eight, including only four heads of families.

For most of the century that followed this wholesale hegira, the people of Tristan became more and more cut off from the outside world. During the eighteen-sixties, the number of American whalers hunting in the Tristan area diminished considerably, owing not only to the general decline of the whaling industry but to a perverse migration of the whales to the vicinity of South Georgia Island, some seventeen hundred miles to the southwest. Then, thanks to the advent of steam, ships of all sorts became independent of the trade winds that had formerly taken them near Tristan. And, as a crowning blow, in 1869 the Suez Canal was opened to shipping, drastically reducing the number of merchantmen everywhere in the South Atlantic.

All this meant, of course, that the Tristan people had fewer and fewer opportunities to barter for the supplies they needed. It also meant that, with the gradual withering away of their island's role as a provisioning center, when they did get a chance to barter they found that homemade garments and hand-carved curios were more in demand than livestock and vegetables. But no matter what they offered, or at what point in their history, some outsiders considered them extremely naïve when it came to striking a bargain. "The islanders have no real idea of values," the Bishop of St. Helena told a reporter after visiting Tristan in 1932. "They will exchange a goose for a shilling knife or for a suit of clothes worth five pounds." On the other hand, as early as 1889 a Captain R. A. Stopford, in command of a British ship that put in at the island, wrote that unless a sharp watch was kept on the Tristan people they would trade only their oldest geese, which were so tough as to be inedible.

Of the pathetically few ships that approached Tristan in the latter half of the century, some proved to be more of a burden than a boon to the community. During the American Civil War, for instance, the Confederate privateer Alabama hove to off Tristan with a Union prize, the Shenandoah, dumped the latter's crew of twenty-seven on the island, despite the hard-pressed inhabitants' protests (which the Tristan people emphasized by running up the British flag), and sailed away. Faced with this *fait accompli*, the islanders lodged and fed the sailors in characteristically kind fashion until a Union gunboat arrived, a few days later, and removed their unwanted guests. Then, too, however much the new trade routes had diverted merchantmen from Tristan, shipwrecks there were not altogether a thing of the past—between the time of the mass migrations in mid-century and the end of the century, fifteen vessels foundered off the island and its two satellites—and these also endangered the continued existence of the community, for whenever necessary the handful of men left to support it would risk their lives to rescue the survivors, and always, no matter how scant their reserves might be at the moment, the inhabitants would shelter and feed the castaways with unstinting generosity until another ship happened by and took them off the island. For these acts of kindness the Tristant people asked nothing in return and usually got nothing.

From time to time, however, the British government, aware of how little the islands could afford such hospitality—particularly since their permanent population was again on the rise—reimbursed them by sending provisions, and even, infrequently, small sums of money with which to buy supplementary supplies from ship captains. In addition, the settlement received a limited amount of material assistance from a succession of Anglican missionaries sent out by the Society for the Propagation of the Gospel in Foreign Parts, the first of whom arrived in 1851—five years before the Widow Glass and her family sailed for New Bedford.

The Society, a London organization, did what it could to raise money among well-wishers in England, but the pickings were lean and the missionaries' contributions to the community were therefore restricted largely to religious instruction and supplying the island children with the rudiments of an education.

The Tristan people needed every bit of outside help they could get, and they never needed it more than in November, 1885, when a longboat in which fifteen of their ablest men were rowing out to barter with a waiting British vessel capsized and all aboard were drowned. Among those lost were the heads of twelve of the nineteen families then on the island—in three of the seven others, the woman of the house was already a widow—leaving the community, which then had a population of ninety-two, with only four grown men, just one of whom was fit to do a day's work, and making its survival contingent on the diligence of its teen-age boys. The British government, upon learning of this catastrophe, reacted in a spirit of generosity hardly comparable to that which was traditionally shown by the Tristan people toward shipwrecked Britishers. After some delay, the Colonial Office forwarded clothing, flour, and other provisions worth about seventy pounds all told, and the Admiralty announced that it would send a warship to Tristan once a year to look into conditions there.

Following one such inspection, in 1892, the captain in charge expressed the belief that the island would eventually have to be evacuated, because it lacked enough men capable of sustaining its population, but he failed to take into account the traditional resiliency of the islanders. Slowly, the community recovered from the blow as its teen-age boys grew older and castaways continued to settle there, among the latter being Andrea Repetto and Gaetano Lavarello, who survived the wreck of an Italian bark in 1893 and founded the Tristan families that now bear their names.

With the outbreak of the Boer War, in 1899, the Admiralty discontinued its annual inspections of the island, and when the fighting ended, three years later, it did not resume them. Instead, the British government again proposed that the islanders move to the Cape. The majority of them, however, refused to consider the idea, and when, in 1907, they declared that they "would rather starve" than leave their homes, the government took them at their word; in fact, for the next decade or so it had little or nothing to do with them, their principal contacts with the mother country being through the Anglican missionaries. After the First World War ended, the government did infrequently arrange for a vessel of some sort to stop at Tristan with supplies and mail, and the Royal Family sent a few gifts, but, aside from whatever radio broadcasts might be picked up on the resident missionary's set, Tristan heard little of "the houtside warld" until 1942, when a meteorological station was established on the island by the Union of South Africa and, later that year, was taken over by the British Navy.

Neglected though the Tristan people had been by their government, the missionaries on the island reported that they remained determinedly patriotic. "People here are very loyal, and Empire Day is a great festival with us," one of them, the Reverend Mr. H. M. Rogers, wrote in an article printed by an English paper in 1922. "The National Anthem, saluting the Flag, a march past of the schoolchildren, three cheers [for the king], and music and dancing figure in the program." Stirred by such dispatches, people back home sent parcels of old clothes and kitchenware to the islanders, but not very many, apparently, for several years later Rogers' wife wrote from the island that "a kettle is a precious possession, to be lent from person to person." During the twenties and thirties, Tristan was so nearly forgotten by the rest of the world that the sighting of a ship off its coast was the occasion for a wild celebration. "Every soul on the island stops work and, screaming 'Ship ho!,' rushes to my house," one of Rogers' successors wrote in the London *News Chronicle* in 1933. "The women pick up their skirts and dance, the men leap in the air and turn somersaults, the children scream, and hundreds of dogs bark frantically." Rogers himself had not thought too highly of the islanders' preoccupation with the sighting of ships. "The men are rather lazy," he told a reporter for a Cape newspaper in 1923. "They live in perpetual hope of a ship coming in with fresh stores, which tends to slow up any work. They promised to build me a church, but after several months they have done very little."

Rogers might as well have said "after several decades," for missionary efforts to get the people of Tristan to build a church dated back at least forty years, to a period when the Reverend Dr. E. H. Dodgson, a brother of the author of "Alice in Wonderland," was stationed there. In 1882, he persuaded the captain of a British Navy vessel to give the community ninety pounds of gunpowder with which to quarry stone for the building, and the project got under way. Several months later, however, the captain of another ship that called at the island estimated that at the rate the work was progressing it would take from twenty to thirty years to complete the church. Evidently, the rate of progress slacked off after that, for the church was not finished until 1923. In 1928, Queen Mary sent a harmonium to be installed in the building, and four years later the *Cape Argus*, while describing it as "a handsome organ," noted that "unfortunately there is no one on the island able to play it." Happily, King George V had come through with a simpler musical gift, consisting of a phonograph and some records, and this was much appreciated by the islanders, whose favorite selection was "The End of the Road," sung by Sir Harry Lauder.

Between the end of the Napoleonic era and the nineteen-forties, as the vicissitudes of an increasingly complex civilization far from their shores first brought the Tristan people into closer contact with the outside world and then left them almost entirely to themselves, their manner of living appears to have remained practically unchanged. In little walled fields, each perhaps a hundred feet square, situated at the southwest end of the small plateau on which the settlement is built and explicitly called the Potato Patches, the men raised the island's staple crop, while their womenfolk—whether at home or walking over to a neighbor's house or even making an excursion on donkeyback—knitted away at great speed, converting the yarn from their spinning wheels into thick, natural-tone pullovers, cardigans, and knee-length stockings, adorned only with thin bands of yarn dyed red and blue. The men, who had once worn blue denim pants and jackets obtained from American whalers, now wore nondescript garments picked up in trade with mariners from many nations, but both they and their women and children were still shod in cowhide moccasins of the kind that Earle's sketch had shown Glass wearing. As in the earlier days of the settlement, the women wore voluminously skirted dresses and headkerchiefs of colorfully printed material, and the little girls wore white Dutch-style headpieces locally called "kapies."

The islanders continued to build their houses along the lines of Glass's, except that they now used blocks of soft volcanic stone—fitted together, without mortar, into walls three feet thick—to make the gable ends, rather than thatching, as in the past. All their houses were laid out along an east-west axis, so that the stone ends might bear the brunt of the violent westerly winds, but apart from this uniform alignment the settlement had no semblance of order, and was innocent of streets. Inside the houses, the sparse furnishings commonly included nautical-style bunk beds and wooden sea chests, these being used both for storage and to sit on. The older houses were distinguishable from the newer ones principally by the fact that in the former whatever little woodwork there was consisted of timbers from ancient shipwrecks, and sometimes there were ship's cabin doors between one room and another, while most of the more modern houses either were without such luxuries or were lined in part with strips of wood from packing cases.

Each year, on a fine morning in March—just before the start of Tristan's April-to-September winter—practically the whole community would sail around Sandy Point, on the east coast of the island, to pick apples in an orchard that had been started by some of the early settlers and that still flourished there. This event, known on the island as Happlin' Day, was a jolly affair, with a picnic lunch under the apple trees as its high point. Just as festive was another event, known as Rattin' Day, which had originated as a serious effort to rid Tristan of a plague of rats and in time became one of the islanders' principal sporting occasions. On Rattin' Day, the men would band together in teams and, with their dogs, head for the Potato Patches, where they would dismantle sections of the stone walls separating the plots and expose nests of rats concealed within. The rats would then be finished off by the dogs while the men stood by to cut off the tails from the remains of the victims, and at the end of the day the team with the most such trophies would be declared the winner. The women and children attended these proceedings as enthusiastic spectators, and around the middle of the day the men would take time out to join them in a picnic on the grass. In the evening, after the last of the rattails had been totted up, there would be a dance—held, in recent years, at a newly built community hall.

July and August—late winter—were planting time in the Patches. The potatoes were harvested in December, January, and February, and while the supply lasted, the islanders consumed them in enormous quantities, boiling them and often eating them "bare"—meaning unsalted and unaccompanied by any other food. While the islanders occasionally slaughtered one of a number of half-tame cattle that grazed among the apple trees at Sandy Point, they were interested in the animals less as sources of beef or milk than as sources of leather for making moccasins. Similarly, the sheep were valued mainly for wool rather than for mutton, and in general meat was eaten only on holidays. The islanders were not, however, averse to varying their diet now and then with certain rather special domestic delicacies. In favorable weather, the men, if they felt so inclined, would set out on foot or in their longboats to hunt for these elsewhere on the island, ranging over or skirting sites they identified by such names as Ridge Where the Goat Jump Off, Down Where the Minister Land His Things, The Ponds Up the East'ard, Noisy Beach, and Deadman's Bay.

Sometimes the men's objective would be an all but barren slope, rising toward the island's summit, where, with their hands, they would kill yellow-nosed albatrosses— known to them as mollymawks, or mollies. Or, in September, during the spring nesting season, they might journey by longboat to a small rookery of rock-hopper penguins near Sandy Point, where they would gather the incubating eggs as a prized form of food and kill some of the adult birds for their fat, which was used both in cooking and as lamp oil. But in time both the penguins and the mollies were pretty well killed off on Tristan itself, and as they became scarcer, the men, during the nesting season, would sail the twenty miles to Nightingale, where there was a very large bird colony. They would stay there for days at a time, living on penguin eggs and the flesh of mollies, and return home laden with enough food to last the community for weeks. In March or April, the men might go back to Nightingale, this time accompanied by several of their hardier womenfolk, to build up their reserves of lamp oil by killing large numbers of penguins and greater shear-waters—birds resembling petrels and called petrels by the Tristan people. The women would render the fat of the prey on the spot, and spend idle moments collecting penguin down to use as stuffing for pillows and mattresses back home.

And, at any season, the men of Tristan—again

provided both the weather and their mood were favorable—
might take to their longboats and go fishing. Here, though,
the idyll was flawed, for in winter, just when the islanders
were beginning to run short of potatoes and were most in
need of fish, it was the weather, far more than the men's
mood, that decided when they could venture offshore, and
the weather then was rarely favorable. Moreover, with the
passing of the years, winter fishing expeditions became increasingly perilous because the longboats engaged in them
were not as sturdy as they had once been. In the days of
recurrent shipwrecks, the Tristan people had been able to
fashion the framework of their craft from salvaged whole
timbers, but by the early nineteen-hundreds they were having to make do with any bits of lumber they could find for
the purpose—even, in some cases, nailing together struts
ripped from packing crates. A piece of driftwood substantial
enough to be made into a keel became a great find on
Tristan, and some of the older islanders still talk with wonder of a log that washed up on the shore back around the
beginning of this century and that they called simply the
Big Tree. Nobody knows where it came from or what kind of
wood it was, but it was a hundred and twenty feet long and
had a maximum circumference of twenty feet. Sawing it up
sparingly, for only the most necessary timbers, the islanders
made it last for twenty years.

In 1876, Captain Lindesay Brine, commander of
the British warship Wolverine and a seafarer with a reflec-
tive turn of mind, if not always a penetratingly observant
eye, wrote after calling at Tristan:

Here we have, in a civilized community, society
reduced to its most elementary form. In fact, the com-

munity exactly fits Herbert Spencer's definition of a simple
society which "forms a single working whole unsubjected
to any other, and of which the parts cooperate with or
without (in this case without) a regulating center." . . .
The islanders render each other voluntary assistance as
occasion demands, but there is no compulsion, neither is
there any jealousy or dissension, envy, hatred or malice, or
any uncharitableness, that could be detected. In case of
variance of opinion the minority submits to the will of the
majority with resignation and self control, and the majority
carries their point without exultation or triumph. . . .
Needless to say, the community is absolutely moral. Living
in honesty, sobriety, and harmony, free apparently from
all crime, vice, dissension, or double dealing, they seem to
have unconsciously carried out the purpose entertained by
the original settler . . . Mr. Jonathan Lambert.

The utopian qualities that Captain Brine saw in
Tristan society were also stressed in the writings of several
of the missionaries who served on the island. Glass was not
only the first governor of Tristan but also the last, and the
community ran itself peacefully along egalitarian lines from
his time on. To be sure, a succession of islanders have borne
the honorary title of "Chief," but this has been used primarily when the people as a whole found it expedient to
be represented by a single spokesman at bartering sessions.
The only real authority recognized by the Tristan people
was that of the father over his family, and it was absolute;
any other pretensions to leadership were alien and repug-
nant to them. (Children were periodically reminded of the
paternal role in the household by bouts of what the islanders
call "hammering.")

Although the islanders' society could be described
as a coöperative one, in most ways it stopped short of
Socialism. The houses, land in active use, most livestock,

and the longboats were privately owned, either by families or—most notably in the case of boats—by groups of men. The island had its rich and its poor; a rich man might own thirty head of cattle, sixty sheep, a score of geese, and a share in a boat, and a poor man only a half share in a cow. Indeed, remarks in the writings of a couple of Tristan missionaries indicate that the island society stopped so far short of Socialism that now and then in winter, when the poorer or less provident members of the community ran out of potatoes and were on the verge of starving, they had to barter precious timbers from their houses with their wealthier neighbors in order to get something to eat—not precisely an example of the "voluntary assistance as occasion demands" that impressed Captain Brine.

Some of the missionaries, and some of the ship captains as well, also saw the community as a slightly tarnished paragon of virtue. The Reverend Mr. Rogers, for example, not content with complaining about the laziness of the men, particularly when it came to building him a church, wrote in the Manchester *Guardian* that the islanders were addicted to cadging supplies from him that he could ill afford to part with, and his wife told a reporter that every time a ship bringing mail from home put in at Tristan, parcels addressed to the Rogerses disappeared on the way from the beach to their house. As for the sobriety of the islanders, which Captain Brine virtually took for granted, some visitors to the community were led to suspect that the people abstained from alcohol only for lack of opportunity to get the stuff. A Captain W. J. P. Pullen, of the British Navy, wrote in 1862 that he was "sorry to believe" that, besides the more humdrum commodities that the islanders acquired from Yankee whalers, they also got "spirits, for some appeared at the close of our stay to be in a rather excited state from something stronger than water." And the Reverend Mr. Dodgson felt obliged to note that "drunkenness, I am sorry to say, has a hold on a few of the men when they get the chance."

Because the islanders supposed that the missionaries were acting more or less on behalf of the British government, as loyal subjects they put up with a lot of what, in view of their traditional scorn for authority, they must have considered nonsense, or worse—since even the best-intentioned missionary believed that the object of his activities was to gently lead his flock in ways he felt would be beneficial to it. But sometimes a missionary would go out of bounds, perhaps by exerting pressure to have his favorite installed as Chief. When such puppet leaders were set up, however, they were largely ignored by the islanders, who continued to carry on in their own haphazard fashion.

As one of the clerics lamented, it was terribly hard to get the men to "pull together." What with the lonely lives led by the solitary missionaries in this remote outpost, and the passive resistance of the islanders to many of their efforts, it is small wonder that, according to the press, one of them, in 1923, was "trembling wth emotion" when he boarded a visiting vessel to enjoy the companionship of its passengers for a few hours, and that five years later another, under the same circumstances, was "wild with excitement" —so much so that, according to a Cape paper, although "divine service could have been held on the ship, [he] was in too nervous a state to conduct it."

As long as the weather station on Tristan was being run as a wartime operation, the British Navy saw to it that the island was adequately supplied, and also employed some of the inhabitants, paying them partly in currency but mostly in chits redeemable for goods at a canteen it had set up. In 1946, however, the Navy pulled out of Tristan, closing the canteen and returning control of the weather station to South Africa (which manned it with a staff of two), and the islanders found themselves pretty much the same forgotten people they had been before the war. Then, three years later, their situation began to change again, this time very considerably, when—largely through the efforts of the Reverend Mr. C. P. Lawrence, an Anglican who had served as a Navy chaplain on Tristan during the war—some South African interests organized the Tristan da Cunha Development Company to fish in the waters around Tristan and to exploit, with the help of local labor, rich beds of crawfish, otherwise known as rock lobsters, lying just off the island. The company built a small canning plant near the settlement, and later a freezing plant to preserve crawfish tails, which, under the name of South African rock-lobster tails (zoologically accurate enough, even for those originating in Tristan waters), have become quite popular in the United States in recent years.

The more able-bodied Tristan fishermen could earn as much as a hundred pounds a year, and the company opened a store where they could spend this cash on food, household goods, and hardware. In 1950, the Colonial Office, which had had a hand in the establishment of the fishing enterprise, in an effort to familiarize the islanders with a few elementary modern techniques, assigned a team of four specialists—an administrator, an agricultural officer, a doctor, and a nurse—to steady duty in the community, meanwhile taking over the company store and providing facilities for post-office savings accounts, in which the islanders were encouraged to salt away some of their earnings.

Although the stubbornly individualistic Tristan people did not take very kindly to the threats to their independence that were raised by these outside influences, even they could see that from a material viewpoint they were decidedly better off. The agricultural officer may have found them indifferent to suggestions that they employ up-to-date methods of grazing and fencing, but they were not so aloof when it came to spending their money on articles designed by a newer civilization to make life easier— kerosene-burning stoves and lamps, for instance, which made it unnecessary for them to scour the island for firewood or hunt penguins and petrels for their oil. "Things were changing all the time—getting more Europeanized," according to Miss Rhoda Downer, an Englishwoman who taught school on the island during the late nineteen-fifties. "The women still wouldn't dream of giving up their heavy knitted stockings in favor of nylons, which were considered rather indecent, but a few of the young girls started buying ankle socks. Sewing machines were selling quite well, along with dress patterns for Sunday clothes, and some of the girls were going in for home perms." Nor was that all. Under the direction of the new administrator, water was piped from a communal spring into the Tristan people's homes, flush toilets were installed, and drainage facilities were introduced, giving the primitive little community on the edge of limbo a sanitation system superior to those of some villages that may still be found in parts of Britain.

Such was the affluent state of society on Tristan, whose population now numbered two hundred and sixty-one persons—apart from a mushrooming British supervisory staff of twenty-one, headed by Peter J. F. Wheeler, who, at thirty-two, was the island's administrator—when, at around noon on August 6, 1961, the inhabitants felt something that was entirely new in their experience: a sudden slight tremor of the ground beneath their feet. It was felt by men working at the Potato Patches, by housewives in the settlement, and, at Sandy Point, almost on the opposite side of the island, by Wheeler and a party under his supervision, who were spending a few days there planting saplings. Wheeler didn't think much about the single tremor until he got back to the settlement about a week later and learned with some concern that four or five additional tremors had been felt there since the first one. (He had felt no others at Sandy Point.)

The disturbances continued to jolt the settlement for about three more weeks, increasing slightly in frequency and intensity, and then they stopped. For a few days, everybody breathed easier, but toward the end of the first week in September the tremors began again, and now their jolts were sharper still. The Tristan people were well aware that their entire island had once been an active volcano, and their uneasiness was not much dispelled by South African seismologists who, in response to radioed reports sent out by Wheeler, advised him that the tremors were probably just a matter of an adjustment in a geological fault along the Mid-Atlantic Ridge and that Tristan's once active volcano was not of a kind given to recurrent flareups.

"I began to be quite conscious of the fact that we were sitting on a ledge with a two-thousand-foot escarpment behind us and only the sea in front of us," Wheeler recalled when he got back to England. "After all, we hadn't so much as sighted a ship in five months. But fortunately the commercial fishing season off Tristan starts around the middle of September, so we knew we could expect a couple of the Development Company's boats to show up pretty soon." The first to arrive was the hundred-and-sixty-four-foot Tristania, and her captain, on coming ashore, was quite perturbed by the violence of the tremors that greeted him.

In the hope of getting some idea of how widespread the disturbances might be, the agricultural officer and three islanders took off aboard the Tristania for Nightingale, where they stayed five days, maintaining a round-the-clock check for tremors there, while a corresponding team kept track of those felt in the settlement. During that time, the settlement team recorded eighty-nine tremors, but, to Wheeler's dismay, when the four men returned from Nightingale they reported that they had felt no tremors at all there. Their report, coupled with the fact that he had felt only one tremor at Sandy Point while the settlement had experienced several, led Wheeler to suspect the worst—that the underground pressures were pinpointed on the plateau. He immediately radioed his fears to the Colonial Office, and asked if it would be possible to send a volcanologist to Tristan on the Tjisadane, a Dutch liner that was sailing soon from Buenos Aires to Cape Town and was due to stop at the island to pick up a British nurse who had completed her tour of duty there. The Colonial Office replied that there wasn't time to assemble enough of the appropriate seismological instruments to make a visit worthwhile, but it conveyed reassurances, much like those Wheeler had received from South Africa, as to the unlikelihood of the Tristan volcano's coming to life again.

As if to confirm this optimistic view, almost simultaneously with the receipt of this message the tremors now subsided—but only for a couple of days. When the shocks began again, they were ominously accompanied by subterranean rumblings and thumpings, and they became progressively more severe, shaking pictures from walls and crockery from shelves. Far worse—potentially, at any rate—they touched off rockslides on the cliff behind the settlement, sending boulders as big as automobiles tumbling down perilously close to some of the dwellings. During the first week in October, the rockfalls occurred at a rate of almost one an hour. As the rocks came hurtling down, they would throw up clouds of dust hundreds of feet high, which sometimes, depending on the direction of the wind, would envelop the whole settlement and, in the daytime, obscure the sun. But alarming though the sight of these repeated slides certainly was, what the islanders found even more unnerving was the sound of the rocks thundering down from the cliff at night, when there was no telling where they might end up. While the Tristaners remained outwardly calm in this time of anxiety, they could not help realizing that they were in serious trouble. As one of them said later, "The people was werry un'appy, because they knew there was something wrong with hisland."

Any lingering doubts that the people may have had were dramatically dispelled on Sunday, October 8th—now commonly referred to by the Tristan people as "the day the harth cracked." In accordance with their Sabbath custom, most of the islanders had attended evensong services in the church, and as they were on their way home those living at the eastern end of the settlement discovered a number of cracks in the earth, extending across the width of the plateau from the base of the escarpment to the sea.

At the time, the cracks were barely discernible where they cut through the turf that covered most of the plateau, and could be clearly distinguished only where they crossed a footpath or wagon track. As the afternoon wore on, however, the cracks gradually widened, breaking underground pipes and causing small jets of water to shoot up all over the settlement. By nightfall, doors in some of the houses near the cracks had to be pried open.

All night, the cracks continued to widen, and during intervals when masses of rock were not crashing down from the cliff, many an islander could hear in his own living room a small imitation of those massive cascades as showers of pebbles, loosened from the masonry of his chimney, rattled out of the fireplace and onto the floor. But there were not many such intervals, and shortly before midnight the rockfalls became so threatening that nearly all the islanders at the eastern end of the settlement, acting in wordless accord, quietly left their homes almost at the same moment and, shouldering sacks full of their possessions or carrying babies in their arms, straggled over to spend the rest of the night with relatives on the western side. Among them were Mrs. Ida Green, who had given birth to a baby four days previously. Mrs. Green moved in with her sister-in-law, Mrs. Rene Green, taking the baby with her, and shortly after she arrived the Reverend Mr. Charles J. Jewell, the island's Anglican minister, who had learned of her move, stopped in to see if mother and child were all right. Finding the mother chiefly concerned because her baby had not been baptized, he set about remedying that situation on the spot; using a pudding bowl as a font, he performed the ceremony amid the furious roar of falling rocks.

By morning, things seemed to be a little better. Some of the east-enders, returning to inspect their homes, found that some of the cracks in the ground had closed up, and that doors that could not be budged the previous night now opened and closed readily. Many of the Tristan people began to express the hope that they had experienced the worst of the disturbances, but their optimism faded at about three o'clock that afternoon, when a crack far wider than any of the earlier ones appeared in the ground about three hundred yards east of the settlement. Wheeler and a few of the island men went to take a look at the new crack, and as they drew near it they saw a section of the ground along its far side start to rise. It rose gently and silently, at a rate of perhaps four inches a minute, until at the end of half an hour or so it attained a height of about ten feet, all the while slowly assuming the shape of a bubble, whose grass-covered surface was severely lacerated with fissures. At one point, a sheep grazing too near the edge of the large crack, which was now a gaping V-shaped trough, fell into it and disappeared. But as the grassy boil continued to rise, the bottom of the trough rose, too, and on it was the sheep, which, upon reaching ground level, scrambled back onto the turf and resumed its grazing.

Hurriedly, Wheeler left the scene and made his way to the center of the settlement, where there hung an old naval shell case, ordinarily used as a gong to summon the islanders on mornings when the sea was deemed safe for fishing. After he had struck this with an iron bar and the men had gathered around, Wheeler told them that they would have to evacuate the settlement the next day, aboard the Tristania, which, fortunately, was standing by off the landing beach. The Tristania would take them to Nightingale Island, he continued, and he advised them to have their womenfolk prepare for the emergency by packing blankets and warm clothing. Next, he got in touch by radio with the Royal Navy, at Cape Town, informed it of the islanders' predicament, and asked for help, since the Tristania and another ship, the much smaller Frances Repetto, did not have the facilities for carrying so many passengers any great distance. The Navy reminded him that the liner Tjisadane was due very soon at the island, and also promised that the frigate H.M.S. Leopard would leave South Africa for Tristan immediately, and that, proceeding at top speed, she should arrive in three or four days.

Toward dusk, Wheeler returned to inspect the earth bubble. He found that it had swelled to a height of perhaps thirty feet and was resting on a base of about the same diameter. Moreover, it was continuing to grow, and, staring at it, Wheeler, though he admittedly knew nothing about such matters, became convinced that he was witnessing the evolution of a new volcano. He went back to the gong, banged it again, and told the men that the settlement would have to be evacuated right away. Because of the impending darkness, however, and because he feared that the bubble might suddenly erupt and flood the landing with lava, he decided against trying to get the islanders into their longboats and out to the Tristania that night; instead, he instructed the men to take their families to the Potato Patches and bed them down there.

In the gathering twilight, the islanders, walking in twos and threes and carrying the things they had packed in the last few hours, set out for the Patches. There some of them slept, or tried to sleep, in little sheds that ordinarily served as bad-weather shelters for the men working in the

fields, and the rest huddled in ditches to escape the full force
of a strong, cold west wind. It was a miserable night for
everybody. In the darkness, the people could hear the roar
of rockfalls from the great cliff, and at each fall the dogs—
nearly every family had one—would set up a furious bark-
ing and the donkeys on the plateau would bray in strident
unison. At about two o'clock, the shivering refugees heard
an exceptionally loud boom, for which they had no ex-
planation until dawn. Then, after making a prearranged
radio contact with the Tristania over a portable transmitter,
Wheeler learned that the bubble had blown open at about
that time and could now, from the ship, be seen pushing hot
boulders and glowing cinders. On hearing this, Wheeler and
a group of Tristan men hastily set out toward the settlement.

They got their first glimpse of the new volcano
from the brow of a hill. "The men run like wild to see what
the wolcano look like, and when they get to the toap of
the hill they stand werry still, just watching it," one member of the group said later. "When I see it, I think, Well,
that's the end of hour hisland." The bubble of grass had
become a cone of lava some seventy feet high, with sul-
phurous-smelling smoke alternately streaming and puffing
from its top while boulders and cinders rolled down its
sides.

The Tristan people's longboats lay drawn up on
the shingle only a couple of hundred yards from the volcano, and Wheeler, more loath than ever to risk herding the
islanders onto the landing beach now that it was practically
at the base of the smoldering heap, directed the men to
row their craft to another beach, near the Patches—one that
was seldom used, because it bordered on a rock-strewn bay

and could be reached from the plateau only by a narrow path leading down the face of a two-hundred-foot cliff. The sea was rough there, and breakers were sweeping across the mouth of the bay, making it difficult for the longboats even to get in to the landing, but after some time one of them managed it, and, having taken aboard a load of elderly persons and mothers carrying babies, successfully got off again, bound for the Tristania. But the second boat to try to reach the landing almost capsized, and it became apparent that the chances of evacuating all the remaining Tristan people from that beach without a disaster were very slim.

Accordingly, Wheeler, reversing his tactics, directed the rowers to return to the regular landing beach, and then called the rest of the islanders together and told them that they would have to proceed there on foot as rapidly as possible; there was no time for them to go back to their home and salvage anything more, he said. Clutching the few possessions they had brought with them, the people patiently turned back, climbed the two-hundred-foot cliff, and made their way from the Potato Patches to the landing beach—past their homes, behind which stood the smoking volcano, whose peak now stood about a hundred and fifty feet above the ground—and waited their turn to clamber aboard the longboats. The sea off the settlement was calm, and by one o'clock in the afternoon every man, woman, and child was safely aboard either the Tristania or the Frances Repetto, which had returned from a fishing trip that morning. As the two ships turned and headed for Nightingale, islanders looking back could see a second bubble of earth beginning to rise in a bog right beside the most easterly house in the settlement.

The refugees spent Tuesday night on the barren

coast of Nightingale. The next morning, their immediate cares vanished when they saw the Tjisadane appear off the island, its mission to pick up one nurse at Tristan now expanded to include picking up all the fugitives from the volcano and taking them on to Cape Town. "By mid-afternoon, everybody was on board," Mr. Jewell noted in his diary that night. "We set sail and as we passed [the settlement] we saw there were now three cones, all emitting smoke and great rocks that rolled down the sides. As people gazed at what had been their homes . . . there were many tears, especially among the older folk."

The British Navy's Leopard reached Tristan three days after the departure of the Tjisadane, and put a landing party ashore to go through each house in the settlement and remove all the portable valuables to the frigate for ultimate return to their owners. The members of the party found that the original bubble (the two others eventually merged with it) was two hundred and forty feet high and still growing. Before leaving the island they rounded up and shot all of the dogs they could find, as a precaution against their going wild and preying on the other domestic animals, which were to be left on the island.

The Tjisadane arrived at Cape Town on October 17th, and the refugees received a warm welcome, for South African newspapers had been printing detailed accounts of their misfortunes. Some of the islanders who had relatives in the vicinity considered settling down with them, but in the end they decided to go along with the majority in accepting an offer from the British government to transport them, as British citizens, to England. (Thereby, they avoided the likelihood of being classified, under South Africa's policy of Apartheid, as "colored" persons and so being segregated, because of the mulattoes from St. Helena among their ancestors.)

Aboard the Stirling Castle, while completing their six-thousand-mile voyage into exile, the Tristan people were given numerous inoculations against the communicable diseases of Western civilization, since few of them had ever been exposed to, and even fewer had contracted, any of these ailments, with the exception of the common cold, which usually beset the settlement after a ship called there. In fact, it was widely assumed at the time, on the basis of what visitors had observed and what the islanders had said about themselves, that the people of Tristan enjoyed almost perfect health—an assumption that failed to stand up once the refugees reached England, where they became subjects of close study by teams of physicians representing the British Medical Research Council. The doctors found that many of them were afflicted with anemia, asthma, and roundworms, and concluded that although in their natural environment they had a somewhat longer life expectancy than Englishmen living in England, they were generally in poorer physical shape. Even the condition of their teeth was disappointing.

In 1937, a group of Norwegian scientists, after a decade of periodically checking up on the islanders, had reported that their teeth "had no more decay than those of ancient man" and that over the ten years covered by the survey "only 1.84 to 3.96 per cent of the teeth were found to be carious"—a fact that was all the more remarkable in view of the islanders' predominantly soft diet. But that was before the canteen was established on the island, providing the community for the first time with a relative abundance of sugar in one form or another. It was discovered in

England that the islanders ate an average of half a pound of sweets a week, and that a third of them had cavities in their teeth. Furthermore, genetic malformations among the islanders, while perhaps less prevalent and extreme than laymen might expect in so inbred a group, were found to exist at more than twice the comparable rate for the population of England as a whole. Some of these abnormalities were of relatively minor nature—lobeless ears, for instance —but others were more serious. Ominously, several islanders were found to be suffering from a congenital abnormality of the eye identified as retinitis pigmentosa, which is marked by progressive retinal changes and deterioration of sight. A recently published report of the Medical Research Council has bluntly warned, in connection with this abnormality, "The incidence of retinitis pigmentosa is of grave significance if the islanders continue as an isolated, inbred community. The genetic implication is a high incidence of blindness in future generations."

The Tristan people's susceptibility to the common cold became all too evident when they reached Pendell Camp, for ninety per cent of them were stricken with it almost at once. In some cases, severe respiratory complications developed, and despite intensive medical treatment four of the older people died. ("The weather didn't help any," Mr. Jewell—who was still with them, living nearby—pointed out at the time. "After all, the islanders came directly from the end of a Tristan winter into the beginning of winter here in England.") Those who remained physically able to get about were shown how to operate the electric stoves and heaters in their quarters (on their island, only the community hall and the installations of the Development Company were equipped with electricity), were told what the duties of a policeman are and how he can be helpful to confused but law-abiding citizens, and were subjected to a series of lectures by civil servants that introduced them to the complexities of the welfare state—social security, unemployment insurance, health and hospitalization services, maternity benefits, and so on.

The newcomers needed considerable help in finding their way around the camp and the countryside, for their natural bewilderment in getting about in a strange setting was compounded by the fact that their sense of direction was still oriented to the sun as it appears in the Southern Hemisphere; when it showed up in the southeast, for example, they took it to be in the northeast and proceeded accordingly. The resulting confusion was particularly galling to them because they, far more than most Westerners, had been brought up to rely on the sun as a guide. At home, their sense of direction was so well developed that they were accustomed to describing the position of objects not in terms of left or right but by their compass position; thus, a Tristan housewife asking her daughter to fetch a thimble from across the room might tell her she would find it "on the heast hend of the shelf, just west of the teapot," and one Tristan man who was being examined by the island doctor on account of a bothersome tooth exclaimed, "No! Not that one, Doctor. The one heast'ard!"

While the Tristaners were struggling to adjust themselves at Pendell, the government was considering the question of their future. According to the few reports it had been receiving about the Tristan volcano, the prospect of their being able to return to the island soon seemed dim. At the end of October, the master of the Tristania reported that the volcano had grown to a height of about four hundred feet and that although only one of the houses in the settlement had been destroyed, the cannery and freezing plant had disappeared beneath a mass of lava. In December, two geologists who had been sent, aboard a British vessel, by the Royal Society to observe the volcano reported that the main crater was throwing "blocks or bombs" a hundred feet into the air, and that lava had overrun the greater part of the landing beach. The Society thereupon announced that it was organizing a full-scale scientific expedition to land on Tristan and make a thorough study of conditions there. The government, while not saying so officially, made it clear that, regardless of the findings of this expedition, it had no enthusiasm at all for reëstablishing a community on Tristan. Early in 1962, the islanders were settled in some houses that had served as family quarters for enlisted men at a former Royal Air Force base at Calshot, on the west bank of the Solent, eighteen miles from Southampton—a semi-industrial region in which oil refineries, chemical plants, and housing developments are spread out between old villages and the chances of getting a job are reasonably good.

Happening to be in England around that time, I paid several calls on the Tristan people in their new homes —rows of small, attached two-story houses of gray stucco, each with its own bay window looking out on its own miniature square of grass, which was enclosed by a trimmed hedge with a gate in it. I soon discovered that it was no easy matter to seek out any particular islander in the community —recently designated as Tristan Close by the post office— since it contained twelve Green families, along with eleven Swain, thirteen Glass, eight Lavarello, seven Repetto, seven

Rogers, and two Hagan families. Furthermore, some of the islanders with the same surname also had the same Christian name, but, confusing though this might seem to an outsider, the residents kept all such identities clear enough among themselves by preceding the Christian names with "Big" and "Little" (denoting seniority) or with the name of a spouse or parent. Thus, there was a Big Gordon Glass in one ramification of the Glass family and a Little Gordon Glass in another; Margaret Repetto, the wife of John Repetto, and her daughter-in-law, another Margaret, who was married to Lindsay Repetto, were called Johnny's Margie and Lindsay's Margie, respectively; and Dick Swain's wife, Margaret, was known as Dick's Maggie, while their unmarried daughter Margaret enjoyed the more formal name of Dick's Margaret.

The islanders' characteristic speaking habit of intruding "H"s before words beginning with vowels and of substituting "W"s for "V"s applied liberally to their pronunciation of their neighbors' names. So, among the men's Christian names, there were h'Adam, h'Allen, h'Albert, and h'Ian, and among the women's and girls' there were h'Isabel, h'Ada, h'Emily, h'Ida, h'Ivy, h'Irene, and even h'Asturias, a thirteen-year-old Repetto girl named after a luxury liner that had occasionally called at Tristan during round-the-world voyages. Where a name or a word began with an aspirate, it was often, but not always, dropped: "Henry" was "Endry," but "Helen" remained "Helen." "Violet" invariably came out "Wiolet," and there were three Wiolets in the community—Granny Mary's Wiolet, Crissy's Wiolet, and Edith's Wiolet.

Like their complexions, the speech of the islanders varied considerably, and there were differences in accent between, say, some of the older people, whose talk could be quite hard for an outsider to understand at first, and some of the younger ones, whose use of archaisms was not nearly so noticeable as that of their elders. But in varying degrees they all talked in a broad-vowelled early-nineteenth-century Southeast yeoman's English ("It do be a foine day," they might say) that was slightly overlaid, perhaps, with the accents of the colored people of St. Helena. The peculiar drawl of the Tristan people gave certain words great character; when they talked about Tristan the word came out "Tri-*ist'n*," like a sigh, and when they said "yes" it could come out either as an acquiescent breath that faded into nothing ("yeaazzzz") or a bright responsive affirmation ("yess" or "yass!").

The language of their English ancestors seemed to have hung on with the Tristan people to the almost complete exclusion of the speech of their forebears of other nationalities. Back in the eighties, the Reverend Dodgson wrote home that the Tristan people "speak English slightly Yankeefied," but the islanders' speech at Calshot retained no such characteristics that I was able to distinguish, except for the use of one or two essentially American words, like "gulch," which they applied to the innumerable ravines that radiate outward and downward from the island peak. A few words were pronounced in a way that sounded slightly Scottish, but without the burr—"fairns" for "ferns," "buds" for "birds" and "wuk" for "work." And the islanders called their home-knitted sweaters "ganseys," a word, still in use in some parts of Scotland and Ireland today, that derives from the name of the island of Guernsey, and that was used by sailors in the last century to describe seamen's sweaters.

I was often reminded that the Tristan people were

descended from shipwrecked mariners when I heard the nautical terms with which their conversation was salted. Among them, string was not called "string;" it was known as "line." And an islander, in recounting how, before the eruption on Tristan, the earth tremors shook loose the large stones in the gable ends of houses in the settlement, did not say that the stones "came apart;" he said that they "come adrift." Also, when Tristan people in Calshot were describing a moderate distance between one object and another on the island, they sometimes measured it in fathoms.

When the Tristan people moved into the Calshot houses, they found that their landlord, the government, had outfitted their quarters with new furniture, crockery, and cutlery, and even with alarm clocks. In a way, the alarm clocks seemed to symbolize the changes that the exiles were having to make in their habitual mode of living. Before long, these changes began to irk a considerable number of them, and what appeared to bother them most about life in England was the tyranny of the timetable. On Tristan, where the men would occasionally wait for weeks before the weather eased enough to allow those who felt like it to go fishing, nobody bothered much about the passage of time, but now, regardless of the weather or personal inclination, everyone had to keep track of the hour, and even the minutes in it. Nearly all the men and single women at Tristan Close had found employment through the local Labour Exchange—the men mainly as building laborers, and the women as workers either in a frozen-poultry plant at Lymington, ten miles away, or on the assembly lines of an electronics factory in the same general area—and that meant getting up at a certain time every weekday morning, catching a bus that ran on a tight schedule, and, as menials subject to discipline by some impersonal authority, toiling the day through until a certain hour at jobs not necessarily of their own choosing. And the timetable, I soon learned, wasn't the only offender in the eyes of the Tristan people.

Paying taxes was another; indeed, this was an even more disagreeable obligation to them than it was to most of their contemporaries, because they had never paid any before. Some of them even grumbled at being charged a shilling to have a prescription filled, as the National Health Service required, instead of receiving their medicine free from the local medical officer, as they had on Tristan, that bleak Arcadia where, in a small way, they had had what many people the world over would like to have—a share in the benefits of a welfare state without the necessity of putting up a penny toward its support. In other islanders, though, I sensed not only resentment but a kind of underlying terror of the society of which they were supposed to become a part. This, I gathered, stemmed largely from a nagging, uneasy awareness that, now that they no longer owned their own homes and had no way of raising or catching their food, they must without fail earn money, week in and week out, to feed and shelter their families. "Our people go around and they feel heverything pressing in on them," one of the men told me. "It's like they tie you in a sack and you hopen your eyes and you don't know where you iss."

There was one aspect of life in England that proved to be particularly strange and disturbing to the islanders—the existence of open violence. After I had been around Calshot for a few days, I learned that the community, in addition to facing its other difficulties, was in distress over the news that Big Gordon Glass, a gray-bearded and very gentle-mannered islander who had lost an arm some years before on Tristan as a result of an accident in the fish cannery, and who had obtained a job in a factory near Southampton as a night watchman, had been robbed while making his rounds one night. The robbers were a couple of Teddy boys, who, after demanding money from the bewildered islander and finding none, had taken his watch out of his pocket and smashed it to pieces on the ground before his eyes. The victim himself was so shaken up by the incident that he took to his bed for several days, and would hardly talk about the matter to anybody.

But in general, with all their problems, the Tristan people seemed to be trying gamely to do what was expected of them and at the same time to live their normal lives as well as they could under the circumstances. Weekdays, once the workers were off to their jobs and the children—there were forty-four of them between the ages of five and fifteen —had boarded buses for schools in the neighboring town of Fawley, Tristan Close became a quiet place. Having done their housework, the womenfolk might go shopping, knitting unconcernedly as they strolled over to the nearby general store, where they bought all of their foodstuffs except meat, fish, and bread, which tradesmen's vans brought to their doors. Possibly because they didn't like the available fish— they missed the fresh flavor of the Tristan catch, they said —the islanders were eating more meat than formerly, most of it of the cheaper types. (A Tristan housewife in Calshot, when told that it smelled as if she was cooking something good in her kitchen, replied, "Yess! I got a sheep's head in the hoven.")

As for bread—once a rare luxury on Tristan, because of the shortage of flour—the women were now buying pre-sliced loaves daily from the Mothers Pride Bread man. At the store, they bought detergents (especially Surf, which was the brand that the island canteen had stocked), canned milk (which they preferred to fresh), and oranges and bananas (novelties to them). But mainly they bought great quantities of their old favorite—potatoes, in hundred-pound sacks. "The older ones who come in here don't know much about handling money yet," the proprietor of the store told me. "They're very trusting. Sometimes they just leave their purses lying on the counter while they look around. And then on the way out they hand them to you and ask you to take out whatever they owe you."

On weekends—and especially on Sunday afternoons, between morning church services and evensong—the inhabitants of Tristan Close kept moving about, drifting into and out of one another's houses ("wisitin'," they called it) in such numbers that the whole community was constantly being reconstituted into new formations. Groups of them would slip silently into one of the small living rooms so rapidly that within a minute the place would be jammed. There they would always be served tea by their hostess, who, depending on her mood, might start chattering or remain absolutely speechless, just staring at the floor. In either case, the visit was likely to end as abruptly as it had begun; one minute the room would be full of people and the next minute the hosts would be sitting there alone, all of their guests having disappeared without, as far as I could detect, any word or gesture of farewell—not even with the "Cheerio" that the islanders ordinarily gave when taking leave of outsiders. But when they encountered each other on the street in the morning, there was usually an exchange of greetings that consisted of the polite question "How you iss?," to which the answer, equally polite, was, if the respondent was well, "I's fresh" or "I's werry fresh," or, sometimes, "I's tight"—a reference to an attack of asthma.

Sociable though the islanders were when together, Tristan Close had a certain ghetto-like air about it, imposed from within. Two or three of the more daring Tristan girls —wearing lipstick and eyeshadow, and even, perhaps, bee-hive hairdos and stiletto heels—were known to have gone with Tristan boys to a dance hall in Fawley, and a few of the Tristan men were in the habit of going over there of an evening, on foot or by bus, for a few beers at the Fawley pub, but otherwise the islanders saw almost nothing of the other inhabitants of the region after working hours, and mingling of their young people with those of the opposite sex outside the community seemed to be discouraged. The Tristan people even remained aloof from the movies, al-though they assured me they had enjoyed the films that had been shown now and then in their community hall on the island, and although at Tristan Close they were only a short bus ride from the nearest motion-picture theatre. The more I saw of them, the more thoroughly convinced I became that their shunning of any company but their own was not merely a reflection of their dissatisfaction with life in England, deep and widespread though this unques-tionably was, but also a reflection of their deep-seated urge to keep their community intact and ready to return, as one man, to the island.

The islanders were quite aware, as they must have been when they lived on Tristan, that they were objects of curiosity, under intensive observation by strangers. When they arrived in England, the press swarmed all over them, and newspaper reporters from the big English dailies were always whisking one or the other family away from Pendell to London so that readers could have exclusive demonstrations, through pictures and words, of the Tristan people's amazement at being shown through a big department store, or the Regent's Park Zoo, or Piccadilly Circus, or the Tower of London, or even a supermarket. Hardly a week went by without a London newspaper's rigging up a new gimmick around the Tristan people, whether it involved a Christmas party, with supposedly the first Santa Claus the islanders had ever seen (the children were represented as being "scared to death" at the sight), or exclusive pictures of the first Tristan baby born in England, together with an interview with the happy mother. On the inspiration of a press agent, Tristan men were lured, for a fee, into constructing a Tristan longboat in public at the annual British Boat Show.

Day after day, Tristan men, women, and children were interviewed before television cameras about their reactions to modern England and everything else. One group of islanders, drawn by lot, were taken to Buckingham Palace, where they made a formal presentation to the Queen of one of the two longboats they had brought with them—more pictures, more stories, more TV interviews. Chief Willie Repetto, the titular headman, was on screen a good deal, and so was Basil Lavarello, a thirty-year-old islander who had previously had some experience of the world outside Tristan as a deckhand on ships in the South Atlantic. One Tristan girl whose voice I heard on a B.B.C. tape was getting to be quite an old hand in front of a microphone, judging by the way in which, at the beginning of the interview, she started right off with "My name is—" and went on fluently from there.

One effect of all the publicity was that the islanders became thoroughly tired of it, and of all the questions put to them about themselves, either by reporters or by English people generally. (Apart from anything else, the very form of direct questioning was a rather alien one to the islanders, who tended to regard it as an intrusion upon their privacy.) A number of the islanders, I discovered, were demanding a fee before they would grant any sort of interview, but I did not take this as necessarily a sign of a simple people's fast corruption by twentieth-century society, because it seemed to fit in with things I had previously gathered in reading about Tristan. During most of this century, for one thing, until the government tried to make the island self-supporting by bringing in the commercial fishery, a good part of the trading in souvenirs and so on that the islanders did aboard visiting ships—sometimes luxury cruise ships— amounted to a kind of begging. And because the islanders, as a people to whom the sighting of a ship had always meant so much, had become accustomed over the years to the idea of receiving meagre but free supplies from missionary societies and other sources of relief, they tended to regard charity as something as natural to their lives as the hardships they had always endured on Tristan. Indeed, just the hardship of rowing their frail longboats through dangerous seas to reach the visiting ships might help to explain this attitude. The mendicant streak among them had no quality of guilt; what begging existed in the community seemed to be regarded as something to be pursued as another island skill, like fishing.

The people occupying No. 14 Tristan Close were one of the twelve Green families at Calshot, and now and again when I was in the neighborhood I stopped in to visit them. The family consisted of Mrs. Sophie Green, a widow in her sixties; her son Harold, twenty-six, who had a job in a boatbuilding yard in Lymington; his wife, Amy, twenty-three; and the young couple's two small children, Richard and Pamela. The first time I called there, late one chilly afternoon, I found them all gathered in the living room, where a coal fire was burning in the grate. Over the fireplace were two alarm clocks—one battered-looking and with a black dial, the other newer-looking, with a red frame. On a table by the bay window stood a vase filled with cheap plastic flowers, and next to the table sat Mrs. Green, a broad-faced woman with her hair drawn back in a bun. She was knitting a sock at a furious pace, as was Amy, a slightly built girl, with somewhat slanting eyes and a sharp nose; between the showers of impatient clickings coming from the women's flashing needles and the slower tickings of the two clocks beating away side by side on the mantelpiece, the place had a wonderfully busy air. Amy's husband, a round-faced, well-built, rather dark-skinned man, was seated beside her, while their children played on the floor.

I offered Mrs. Green my sympathy about the death of her husband. "Yeaass," Mrs. Green said. "He passed away just two weeks to the day after we get to Pendell Camp. It wus a shock and a blow. It wus a blow for me because we wus just come to the houtside warld, which we don't know nothing about. It wus all so strange. It seemed werry strange when we fusst come here, but we get a warm welcome. It wus real strange. We hear a lot about h'England on the hisland, but we didn't know if all the things we hear is true."

I tried to get some idea from Harold of what the islanders had expected England to be like.

"All we know about the houtside warld wus we had to wuk," he told me. "We knew if you got no money on the houtside you went hungry. On Tristan, if you got no money you don't need it. Everything you want here you got to buy, and we ain't used to it, you see. On Tristan, we don't have no income tax and we don't pay no rent, because we all has our own houses. On Tristan, when you want to wuk, you wuk. If you don't want to wuk, you don't wuk. You can lie in bed all day if you feels like it. Here I got only one job, but on Tristan I got all different jobs. One day I can go farming, another day I can go to the horchard, another day I can go to Nightingale for buds. And when I want to fish, I can get as many fish in five minutes as I can carry away. *Fresh* fish, too."

"On Tristan, you got all the potatoes you want," Amy said. "Potatoes is so expensive here—thirty-six shillings a hundredweight."

I asked Harold if he was really unhappy in England, and he replied, "I wus happier on Tristan. We got dances there, but we haven't felt werry good to have dances yet in England."

"Me and Harold went to Southampton once," Amy said. "We didn't like it at all. There's too much traffic. We bought those flehrs there." She indicated the vase on the table.

"A home without flehrs is like no home at all," Mrs. Green said. "Every house on Tristan has flehrs."

"Southampton is nothing to what Cape Town iss,"

Harold said. "We stop in Cape Town a few days on our way to h'England. Cape Town to us wus the beautifullest place we ever see. A friend took us on toap at night. It wus just like stars out, all over. In one of the big shops I see in Cape Town they got a hescalator. I never seen that in h'England. A hescalator is a ladder and when you step on it it turn round and round and it takes you right up to where you want to go. If you get your toes in it, it'll cut your toes off. When it come to the level of the platform, you *got* to step off. Really lovely!"

"Once in h'England we wus taken up in a bus to the sarcus," Amy said.

"Yess!" Harold said. "And a man came out and throws knives all around a lady"—a big, interested smile—"but he never touched the lady! Hany hanimals they got in the warld there! They got bulldogs playing football. That's the best thing I see in h'England, the sarcus." And he and Amy told how the islanders didn't have to pay to get in to see the show; somebody took them.

I asked Harold whether he had been on a train in England yet. He replied that he hadn't so far. "I seen one, but I ain't been on one," he said. Mrs. Green said, "I ain't seen a train yet." I urged Harold to tell his mother what a train looked like. "A train is the same as a bus, but it goes by steam. It can't go all over the road like a coach—it got to go on the railways," Harold said to her. "I seen one in pictures, but I ain't *seen* one," Mrs. Green said.

I asked how they felt about returning to Tristan.

"The people don't want to go back if the hisland ain't fit," Mrs. Green replied cautiously. "But if the wolcano die down, then the people wouldn't want to stay in h'England."

"I'd go back any day if I had a chance," Amy said, with a big smile. "I don't think there's so much enjoyment here than what there is on Tristan."

"When the day come for Tristan, I don't think there'll be one family what will stop," Harold said, his eyes bright. "That's all what the people talk about—getting back to Tristan. That's what they talk about in the bus going to wuk in the morning and that's what they talk about coming back in the bus at night. I know with the freezing plant gone it would be harder living on Tristan than when we left—at least, for a year or two. But even if the outside *don't* step in and run things again—with the administrator and doctor and schoolteacher and padre— the people won't starve. Tristan would be just the way it wus before I was born."

Wherever I went among the islanders at Calshot, I found the same pervading nostalgia, the same yearnings for Tristan, that I found among the Greens at No. 14. Islanders were always remarking on what they would be doing now on Tristan rather than in England. One evening, I was standing in front of the general store at Calshot with a couple of islanders, waiting for a bus, when one of them, a man in his thirties, pointed to a pile of apples in the store window. "Oan Trist'n, it's just about the time for the happlin' at Sandy Point," he said. "You don't have to buy no happles on Trist'n. They's just lyin' there, nobody to heat them but the rats. The rats is goin' to be fat this year." Another islander would tell me how "it's just about the time for takin' the mollies and the penguin heggs on Nightingale." It seemed as though anything could set the people off about Tristan. Once, a young Tristan man, while walking around the edge of camp with me, looked toward the waters of the Solent, perhaps half a mile away, and remarked, "I ain't seen a whale since I been yere. Not a single one."

A pious group, the Tristan people at Calshot believed steadfastly that God intended them to return to their island and that it was only a matter of time before they would start back. Meanwhile, they did what they could to hasten fulfillment of the divine intention. When the expedition sent by the Royal Society to Tristan got back to London, in April, 1962, it announced that the island's 1961 volcano was of an "extremely quiet type" and now appeared to have subsided almost to the point of extinction. However, Dr. Ian G. Gass, the leader of the expedition, told the press that he and his colleagues had found evidence that several other relatively minor volcanic disturbances, previously unrecorded, had occurred on Tristan in the past—one of them apparently no more than two or three centuries ago—indicating that the island was more volcanically active than had been supposed. In view of this, Dr. Gass expressed the opinion that resettling Tristan would involve some risk —how much risk no one could say with certainty.

The government considered the presence of any risk at all excuse enough to write off a return to the island as a dead issue, but not the Tristan people. The details of the expedition's findings were explained to them at a meeting in Calshot, and its frustrating implications so outraged them that when the Reverend Jewell, who had loyally stuck with them ever since the flight from the island ("Oh, we love our padre, we do," Mrs. Sophie Green had told me), tried to soothe them, some of them, for all their piety, went so far as to boo him.

The islanders held on as obdurately as ever to their determination to make Tristan their home again, and after a great deal of indignant discussion among themselves they drew up a petition to the Colonial Office pleading that they be allowed to go back there. Originally a semi-literate document, the petition was translated by an English sympathizer into language suitable for official consideration and was presented, in legible form, to the proper authorities. The English newspapers, which had been carrying stories from time to time about the islanders, stepped up publicity about them, and Chief Willie was interviewed by reporters about the terrible English weather and the unanimous desire of the community to return to the island.

In midsummer, the British government reluctantly began to yield to the islanders, and announced that it would assist twelve of them to return to Tristan to see for themselves if the place was really habitable, to find out whether the winter storms might not have broken up the lava field sufficiently to make the landing area reasonably usable again, and to plant, if they wished, a new crop in the Potato Patches. The twelve men departed in August, and after they arrived back in Tristan, in the company of an official observer from the Colonial Office, they soon reported, as everyone in Calshot had expected them to, that the place was perfectly fit for the community's return.

In December, the Colonial Office, capitulating further in the face of this development and of continued and well-publicized complaints from the Tristan people in Calshot, held a secret referendum among the islanders in England on the question of their desire to return to Tristan. Everyone over twenty-one was allowed to take part in the balloting, and the result was a vote of a hundred and forty-eight to five for a return to Tristan.

Under the circumstances the Colonial Office had only one course of action left to it, and preparations were made to colonize Tristan all over again. On March 17th, an advance party of fifty-one islanders left the Tilbury docks aboard the liner Amazon for Rio de Janeiro, where they were to be transferred to a freighter that would take them to Tristan; the rest of the islanders were to follow in the fall. The advance party included islanders of all ages. "Girls who arrived wearing shapeless dresses and stockings of white wool are returning with a definite metropolitan gloss—some had nylons and stiletto heels, and carried handbags, transistor radios, and, in one case, a record-player," the London *Times* reported from Tilbury on the day of departure. A large number of reporters and photographers had turned up to record the occasion. "Don't look at the camera, wave to someone on shore," one photographer shouted at a family group lined up on deck a few minutes before sailing time. An old woman in the group, Tristan-blunt to the end, put him straight there and then. "There is no one on shore," she said. The advance party was headed, according to the reporters, by Chief Willie. "Money, money, money, worry, worry, worry all the time," he told the press in an on-deck valedictory.

In November, 1963, the rest of the refugees, save a dozen or so who finally chose to remain in England, sailed from Southampton aboard a Danish ship, the Bornholm, for Tristan. Their departure was given only minor attention in the British press. "Asked why they were returning, most of the Tristans would say little," a newspaper reported. "One replied, 'Well, home is home.'"

To
The
Cytherean
Phase

The space age has come upon us with such suddenness that comparatively few people have as yet accustomed themselves to what seems to me to be its real vocabulary. When I mention "its real vocabulary," I am not referring to the popular language used by broadcasters, by news writers, and by the new breed of middlemen upon whom the first two groups are largely dependent for information about space travel— the Government press agents of Mercury Control and the like who preside by microphone over news coverage of important launchings, and other quasi-scientific sources. Largely through the efforts of the middlemen and popularizers, scientific explorations into space tend to be written about in the Astronaut-John-Glenn jargon of "A-O.K." and "fly by wire," which has the sound of "real space language" but actually is far from being such.

The real language of space, which I believe has been largely degraded before it has had a chance to reach *the intelligent layman, is imbued with a great and logical beauty. It may be a difficult language to accustom oneself to, but much of what makes it at first unfamiliar also makes it attractive, for the concepts it deals with are elegant ones, and the events the language describes occur on such a vast scale that its detached nature has at once a delicate and exalted quality. The language of space is a great leveler; it treats all heavenly bodies according to the same laws, and the reader who becomes accustomed to the concepts it deals with finds that, by being freed from normal earth-bound descriptive processes, his perspective on heavenly bodies, including Earth itself, is affected. Thus, if he is concerned with events within the solar system, he finds that he is able, through the language of space, to dart at will from his usual viewpoint on the revolving Earth and to assume new moving or stationary positions millions of miles away in space, from which he can view Earth and its fellow planets in their respective motions around the Sun.*

Within not such a long time, it seems to me, explorations into space will bring about as profound a change in our outlook on ourselves as the Copernican, Darwinian, and Freudian theories have done in the past. For the present, of course, most of our space explorations, including those scientific probes sent toward the Moon, have been confined to the vicinity of Earth. But a notable exception was the successful mission of the unmanned spacecraft Mariner 2, in 1962, from Earth to Venus, in order to send back information on the conditions of our nearest planetary neighbor. The space vehicle used in this mission is a relatively simple prototype of what will be a series of increasingly complex unmanned space machines—unmanned, that is, by people aboard them. Such machines as Mariner 2 are by no means the anthropomechanical creatures they have been popularly portrayed. There is nothing purposive about their behavior; they are merely slave computing and engineering systems that are ejected into space to act as extensions of the senses of their designers.

In the following piece I have tried—not so much for the sake of conveying scientific information about Venus, but for the sake of attempting to convey some of the concepts and the peculiar grace of the astronomical and technical language involved—to describe that mission. And I have tried to do so from within the general framework of the language of space, rather than from outside it, in the hope that the reader will find this language fitting to the theme.

On August 27, 1962, a spacecraft bearing a number of scientific instruments was launched from the Atlantic Missile Range at Cape Canaveral—now Cape Kennedy—Florida, into the first phase of an interplanetary trajectory designed to bring it into the vicinity of Venus some four months later. The principal purpose of the mission was to collect information on the physical nature of the planet. Notwithstanding studies that had been made for centuries of Venus, the closest planetary neighbor to Earth, up until 1962 very little indisputable scientific information about it had been gathered except that concerning its periodicity. Venus, which since the early part of this century has been known to have about four-fifths of the mass of Earth, lies in orbit between Earth and the Sun at an average distance from the Sun of 67.2 million miles. Its average speed around the Sun is 78,300 miles an hour, and it orbits the Sun in an annual, or sidereal, period of 225 days, during which it comes within 26.3 million miles of Earth at its closest approach, or inferior conjunction. (At superior conjunction, when the two planets are farthest away from each other, with Earth and Venus on opposite sides of the Sun, Venus is 162 million miles from Earth.)

Next to the Sun and Moon, Venus is the brightest object in the sky. Its brightness is due partly to the proximity of the planet to the Sun and partly to the reflection from a very dense cloud layer that covers its surface. Because of the existence of the cloud layer, which has changeable light and dark markings apparently indicating irregular cloud breaks, it had been impossible to determine with any certainty a number of basic facts about the planet, such as its axis, its rate of rotation, and the temperature and structure of its surface and atmosphere. Comparatively recent radar studies made from Earth had suggested that the planet rotated on its axis once every 250 days. Temperatures of 38 degrees below zero, Fahrenheit, had been recorded from Earth from somewhere in the atmosphere of Venus, and temperatures of 615 above zero—approximately the melting point of lead—were believed to exist at or near the surface, but there had been no agreement as to the altitude at which these temperatures existed. One theory had been that the apparent temperatures measured on Venus did not represent true thermal conditions on the surface but were actually the product of a very dense ionosphere around the planet. Another theory held that the high temperatures did exist and were caused by the so-called "greenhouse effect," in which the Sun's rays are trapped within the cloud cover; a third theory had been that the apparent high surface temperatures were due to friction caused by high winds and sand or dust clouds. Other theories variously suggested that the surface of Venus resembled a swamp, an ocean containing carbonated water, or an oil-covered desert.

To obtain data that might assist in providing answers to these and other questions about the true nature of Venus, including the question of whether the temperatures on the planet make it possible for any life to exist there, the spacecraft launched on August 27 bore equipment for two scientific experiments designed to obtain measurements relating to the temperatures of the planet's surface and atmosphere and details of its cloud layer, and four others relating to conditions both in the vicinity of the planet and in interplanetary space: information on magnetic fields, the intensity and distribution of charged particles, and the density and direction of cosmic dust encountered. The spacecraft was also equipped with the means of transmitting back to Earth by radio, over the great distances of interplanetary space, data it collected en route and in the vicinity of Venus.

The spacecraft was not aimed at Venus itself—if it were to enter the atmosphere of the planet it would probably cease to function—but at a roughly triangular area lying in a radius of between 10,000 and 35,000 miles of the sunlit side of the planet and several thousand miles below its equator. To enter that target area the spacecraft would have to travel 181.9 million miles through interplanetary space for a period of 109.5 days. During its journey it would be exposed for a prolonged period to extremes of temperature and to more or less unknown radiation conditions. It would also encounter an unknown amount of cosmic dust and debris; and through all this it would have to keep its scientific experiments and radio transmitter in operating order to the very end; for if the spacecraft were to keep up its transmissions during every hour of its four-month journey but the last, the mission would be a failure.

The launching of August 27 was the second attempt by the United States, under the Mariner program of unmanned interplanetary exploration, to send a spacecraft to the area of Venus. On July 22, 1962, a spacecraft of the same design as the one launched on August 27 was launched from Cape Canaveral. However, after a short flight during which its course became erratic, the vehicle was destroyed by remote control. The failure was caused by two imperfections, the first being an improper working of the airborne rocket's radio equipment, and the second a failure of ground equipment which had been processing the missile's telemetry data to pass on to ground computers a hyphen in a guidance equation, as a result of which erroneous steering commands were sent out to the missile from the computers.

Three times prior to the American launching on August 27, the Russians had tried for Venus and had had their difficulties. The first attempt was on February 4, 1961, when the Soviets managed to launch a spacecraft into a circular or parking orbit around the earth. However, the spacecraft could not be ejected, as planned, from its parking orbit into an interplanetary trajectory. Eight days later, on February 12, 1961, the Russians tried again, this time with partial success. They placed a spacecraft into a planet-to-planet trajectory—the first time in history that such a thing had been accomplished—toward Venus. But after the spacecraft had travelled about 4.5 million miles from earth its radio power apparently failed, and it was heard from no more. And on August 25 of the same year, the Russians made a third attempt at Venus, but as with their first, their spacecraft apparently could not be brought out of its parking orbit.

Launching a spacecraft to Venus is theoretically possible on any day of any year, but for practical purposes, where present American and Russian efforts at interplanetary exploration are concerned, it can be carried out only during certain short intervals before the time when, every 19.2 months, Venus and Earth are at inferior conjunction. A launch is feasible during these intervals for three main reasons: the energy required to throw the spacecraft into its proper interplanetary trajectory is broadly at a minimum (at the actual time of inferior conjunction the required energy is very high); the distance the spacecraft has to travel is also generally at a minimum, which reduces the hazards it will be exposed to in space; and the difficulties of maintaining communication with the spacecraft are also reduced. Every Russian and American launch has been carried out during one of these periods.

The task of calculating a spacecraft trajectory to Venus is very intricate even for those times when the planets are within the area of close approach. Along the general plane of the ecliptic— the great invisible wheel in the solar system of which the Sun is the hub and the Earth's orbital path a slightly elliptical rim around it—the path of Venus lies as a smaller wheel centered on the same hub. The orbital path of Venus is tilted at an angle of less than three and a half degrees from Earth's; the two orbits thus lie in the solar system like two huge, invisible gyroscopes, one smaller, one larger, superimposed on one another around the same center, the Sun, yet canted at slightly different angles of spin. For a spacecraft from Earth to reach a set target area in the vicinity of Venus, it must ordinarily follow a three-dimensional trajectory that takes it not only inward in a precise course from the orbital path of Earth around the Sun but also upward or downward in celestial latitude to intercept Venus as Venus proceeds in its sloping path through Earth's orbital plane. The planned trajectory must take into account as precisely as possible: the energy that can be imparted to the spacecraft by the various components of its launch vehicle, according to the mass of the spacecraft and the launch vehicle's aerodynamics; the point of launch and target area in latitude and longitude, terrestrial and celestial; the velocities and positions of the spacecraft in its various stages of controlled and ballistic flight; the spin of Earth on its axis; the velocities of Earth and of Venus in their orbital paths; the shifting relative positions of the inner planets of the solar system in terms of both their orbital motions about the Sun as a whole and their calculated motions from the time of launch through and beyond Venus encounter; and the gravitational forces of Earth, of the Moon, of Venus, Mars, Jupiter, and the Sun, as they all interact upon themselves and upon the spacecraft through the various phases of flight. The accuracy of the trajectory would be subjected to such uncertainties as the possible imprecision of the calculated Astronomical Unit (the mean distance between the Sun and Earth—about 93 million miles); the possibility of very slight errors in the calculated positions of spacecraft tracking stations in the United States, South Africa, and Australia, and their calculated distances from the center of Earth; and the as yet imperfect knowledge of the various solar and planetary gravitational fields.

Complex as these calculations are, computations of an Earth-Venus trajectory is essentially an exercise in celestial mechanics in which Newton's laws of motion and of conservation of energy, rather than the relativistic formulations of Einstein, are applicable. Newton's laws still satisfactorily explain the relative motions of the planets except in a few special cases, such as a component of the motion of Mercury at its closest approach to the Sun, which can be accounted for only by an application of Einstein's General Theory of Relativity. An adequate trajectory for a spacecraft travelling from Earth to Mercury would thus have to include certain relativistic corrections, but such corrections in an Earth-Venus trajectory are too small to be worth practical consideration. However, such newly discovered forces in space as the very slight but definite pressure exerted on a spacecraft by the stream of gas particles boiling off the surface of the Sun and flowing outward into space—the so-called solar wind—must be taken into account when computing the trajectory for an interplanetary flight; even the light from the Sun possesses a mass and exerts a certain calculable pressure upon objects in space. The trajectory for the spacecraft launched on August 27 included an offset of 8,000 miles to compensate for the expected deflection of the spacecraft from its target by the pressure of the solar wind upon it during the voyage.

The spacecraft launched by the United States on August 27 bore the name Mariner 2, the name Mariner 1 having been given to the spacecraft unsuccessfully launched on July 22. Like Mariner 1, Mariner 2 was designed and assembled by the Jet Propulsion Laboratory of the California Institute of Technology, in Pasadena, California, under contract to the National Aeronautics and Space Administration. The Jet Propulsion Laboratory has overall responsibility under N.A.S.A. for the Mariner missions, including the operation of a central flight control headquarters and coordination of an international ground communications and tracking network known as the Deep Space Instrumentation Facility, which has three primary stations: at Goldstone, California; near Johannesburg, in the Union of South Africa; and at Woomera, in Northwest Australia.

In shape, Mariner consists of a hexagonal tubular base that houses a variety of equipment, and a tubular superstructure that tapers upward from the base in generally conical fashion, with a cylindrical omnidirectional radio antenna at its apex. Around the sides of the hexagonal base six modules of equipment are fitted. They are: the electronic equipment of an attitude control system, for regulating the attitude of the spacecraft during flight; an electric battery and power system; a data encoder for preparing for transmission to Earth information gathered or generated by the spacecraft during interplanetary flight; a command subsystem for relaying maneuvering or switching instructions to the spacecraft from Earth; and a miniature digital central computer and sequencer, the basic regulator of nearly all the functions carried out by the spacecraft during flight.

The hexagonal framework carries, at various points, photoelectric sun sensors used for orienting the attitude of the spacecraft in flight, and the framework and its superstructure also carry a set of gas jets operated by the attitude control system, for manipulating the craft's attitude. On opposite sides of the hexagonal framework are two solar panels, each bearing a large array of photoelectric cells designed to catch, during interplanetary flight, solar radiation and convert it into electricity for the space-craft's power system. The solar panels, which are each five feet nine inches long, are mounted on hinges and are folded, in their launch positions, up against the tapering sides of the spacecraft, where they are held in place by locking devices. The solar panels carry, besides their solar cells, secondary sun senors, and one panel also carries a small antenna for receiving ground commands.

At the bottom of the hexagonal base a small, liquid-fuel rocket motor for making an in-flight, or mid-course, correction of the trajectory is worked into the structure, and at launch position the downward-pointing jet vane of this motor is covered by a movable dish-shaped parabolic directional, or high-gain, antenna, which is at-tached to one side of the hexagonal frame by a motor-driven hinge. The high-gain antenna bears, on one edge of its dish, a long-range optical Earth sensor, for use in orienting the position of the high-gain antenna and the spacecraft itself in relation to Earth during flight. Equip-ment for the various scientific experiments planned—a microwave and an infrared radiometer, a magnetometer, an ion chamber, and instruments for detecting solar plasma, cosmic dust, and the flux of charged particles—is located in various parts of the spacecraft. Altogether, the space-craft weighs 447 pounds, of which only 41 pounds represent the weight of the actual scientific experimental equipment on board. The spacecraft stands 9 feet 11 inches high, and in its launch position, with solar panels folded, is five feet in diameter at the broadest part of its hexagonal base. At the time of launch the whole spacecraft is encased in a conical metal aerodynamic shroud.

The launching of Mariner 2 was first scheduled for

August 17, 1962, 26 days after that of Mariner 1. But a series of technical problems with the launch vehicle, an Atlas-D booster bearing a second-stage, Agena-B rocket, on top of which rested the shrouded Mariner 2, caused the launching to be postponed twice. The first postponement was caused by a failure in the autopilot system of the Atlas, and the launch date was rescheduled for August 26. The second delay was caused by the discovery, early in the launch countdown on August 25, of a battery short circuit in the Agena. The battery was replaced and the countdown was resumed shortly before darkness on August 26, with a new prospective launch time of 5:15 A.M. Greenwich Mean Time on August 27.

The prospective hour and minute of launch were important factors in calculations of the spacecraft's trajectory. On any date offering opportunity for a Venus launch, the geometry of the trajectory imposes a limited period of several hours in which the launch point is brought around by the rotation of the Earth into a position from which the spacecraft can be put into its permissible path. Additional factors, such as the necessity for keeping the launch vehicle well away from land areas during the preliminary phases of flight, and keeping the vehicle within range of tracking stations, further restrict such a launching period to about two hours. This limited period of launch opportunity for a particular target in space during any day is known as a "launch window." Not only is any launching outside of this time window impractical, but within the window itself every second of delay between the scheduled and actual launch times requires that certain modifications, as calculated by ground guidance computers, be made in the trajectory of the launch vehicle.

The launch window for the rescheduled launch of Mariner 2 early on August 27 was two hours and one minute in length, and the launch had been scheduled for the earliest minute in the window—5:15 A.M. But three unscheduled holds in the countdown delayed the final part of the preparations, and it was not until all but 22 minutes of the launch window had elapsed that a fourth try at finishing the countdown was successful.

With its launch vehicle, Mariner 2 rose vertically from the ground at 6:53 A.M. Greenwich Mean Time, and pitched over on an azimuth of 106.8 degrees from true North to enter the first of the three phases of its interplanetary path: the geocentric, an elliptical-circular-hyperbolic trajectory phase departing from the Earth; the heliocentric, an elliptical trajectory phase under the influence of the Sun; and the Cytherean, a hyperbolic trajectory phase approaching and departing from Venus. At the moment of launch, the estimated time of arrival of the spacecraft in the target area on the sunlit side of Venus was December 14, at exactly 3 P.M. Greenwich Mean Time.

Accelerating rapidly in its ascending path, Mariner 2 and its launch vehicle passed through, in turn, the atmospheric layers of troposphere and stratosphere, and two minutes after liftoff were well in the ionosphere, which begins at an altitude of 50 miles. There, upon receiving a series of signals from the ground guidance system, the launch vehicle began to discard engines that now, with their fuel used up, existed only as impediments to its required increase in velocity. First, two booster engines of the Atlas, which lay athwart a third engine known as the sustainer engine, were shut off and were separated by a prepared mechanism from the Atlas, to fall downward and burn up in the dense atmosphere below. Then the sustainer engine, after burning for a few dozen seconds longer, shut off, and the arched path of the vehicle levelled off toward the horizontal.

Approximately four minutes after liftoff, upon a signal from the ground, the conical aerodynamic shroud covering Mariner 2 itself was jettisoned by spring-loaded bolts, and approximately one minute after this occurred the Atlas was separated from the second-stage rocket, so that the spacecraft remained coupled only to the Agena B. Less than a minute after the separation of the Atlas, the Agena B pitched down from its attitude, approximately 15 degrees above the local horizon, to an attitude approximately level with the local horizon. The motor of the Agena B then ignited and burned for a little less than two and a half minutes, during which time the rocket and spacecraft accelerated to a speed required to put them for a short time in a circular, parking orbit around the Earth.

The purpose of the parking orbit was to compensate for the geometrical difficulties imposed upon the mission by the location of the launching point, Cape Canaveral, on the Earth's surface. The flight plan for Mariner 2 called for the spacecraft to be transferred by the Agena B in a circular orbital plane to a point in the South Atlantic approximately over Ascension Island. There, at a certain instant, the Agena B, acting as a sort of mobile launching platform in the ionosphere, was to fire the spacecraft at escape velocity into its interplanetary path away from Earth.

Mated to the Agena B, Mariner 2 entered its parking orbit very nearly according to plan. Computation of the conditions under which it did so were carried out by a Central Computing Center at the Jet Propulsion Laboratory in Pasadena, on the basis of detailed information fed in from instant to instant by radar tracking stations of the Atlantic Missile Range. Among the various computations made were those for the orbital elements of the vehicle's parking orbit —astronomical elements that, in their very abstractness, somehow convey the beauty and symmetry of the flight path:

In hours, minutes, and seconds in Greenwich Mean (Universal) Time, the epoch, or starting time, at which the osculating conic was calculated.

In kilometers, the semi-major axis of the conic section.

The eccentricity of the conic section.

In degrees, the inclination, or angle between the orbital plane and the Earth's (instantaneous) equator.

In degrees, the argument of perigee—the angle, in the orbital plane, eastward from the ascending node to the perigee point.

In degrees, measured from the vernal equinox of the launch date in the instantaneous equatorial plane, the right ascension of the ascending node.

In degrees, measured eastward, at epoch, the true anomaly plus argument of perigee—the angle measured in the orbital plane between the ascending node and the spacecraft.

The cutoff of the Agena B engine took place according to a series of commands that had been passed on to the Agena from the internal communications system of the Atlas just prior to the separation of the Atlas—the latter having received these commands from ground computers prior and up to launch time and having stored them for a required period of time. The cutoff occurred when the internal control system of the Agena B indicated that the second stage had accelerated to a required orbital velocity of approximately 18,000 miles an hour. The Agena B vehicle entered its parking orbit at an altitude of 115 statute miles, in just a little more than five minutes after launch time, and it coasted in this orbital plane for slightly more than 13 minutes. Then, at an instant predetermined by information that had been fed into its internal guidance system by ground computers at launch, and stored there since then, the Agena B motor burned a second time, and accelerated itself and Mariner 2 as one unit. As the velocity of the vehicle increased, its orbit was transformed, in accordance with Newtonian laws, from a circular to a hyperbolic one leading away from the Earth. Two minutes after the second Agena ignition, Mariner 2, still mated to the Agena B, was accelerated on an escape trajectory at 25,700 miles an hour. At this point the Agena B engine was cut off and the Agena B separated from Mariner by the action of spring-loaded bolts. Then, upon command of its internal communications system, the Agena turned sideways 140 degrees in the local horizontal plane of Earth and its unused fuel supply was ejected through small jets, causing the Agena to move into a different trajectory. The purpose of this maneuver was to prevent the Agena B from closely following Mariner 2 in its interplanetary path in such a manner as to cause the spacecraft's optical sensing equipment to mistake sunlight reflected from the castoff carcass of the Agena for either the Sun or Earth and thus interfere with its ability to orient itself in interplanetary flight.

Unburdened by the last stage of the launch vehicle, Mariner 2 was now travelling alone in its flight path—a new, small object soaring within the solar system, endowed now like a miniature planet with its own annual period around the Sun and, like a planet, even possessing, in relation to its mass, a gravitational field of its own. According to preliminary tracking data, on its entry into space the spacecraft was travelling at a speed and in a direction corresponding within close limits to that planned for the first phase of its interplanetary trajectory.

To consider the trajectory from the time of launch forward to the time of encounter with Venus, the relative longitudinal motions for the three objects, Earth, Venus, and the spacecraft were expected to work out generally as follows:

As they might be seen from above the celestial sphere, Earth and Venus, each travelling counterclockwise in its particular orbital path around the Sun, were so placed on the day of launch that Earth was proceeding ahead of Venus and at a distance from it of 65 million miles. But Venus, in its inner orbit, was travelling faster—actually an average of 12,000 miles an hour faster—than Earth in Earth's average motion of 66,000 miles an hour around the Sun. If the paths of the two planets could be traced forward to their respective positions on the date of predicted closest approach to Venus by Mariner 2, the order of precession would be reversed. Venus, in the intervening 109.5 days, would have traversed a little less than half of its period around the Sun, and in the process would have overtaken Earth, which would have covered a little more than a third of its own yearly period. And Venus, travelling in advance of Earth, would be 35 million miles away from it.

To be brought to the vicinity of Venus ahead of Earth on the date of encounter, Mariner 2 was not injected into its interplanetary trajectory at a point ahead of Earth in its motion around the Sun, as one might reasonably expect. Rather, it was injected into its transfer orbit at an instant and at a point in space calculated to send it in a direction precisely opposite to that of the Earth in its motion around the Sun. At injection, the spacecraft was travelling away from Earth on the inner edge of Earth's just-travelled path at a velocity of 25,700 miles an hour. To measure this retrograde speed against the co-existing forward speed that the spacecraft had been endowed with by Earth's motion around the Sun—a motion, at the time of launch, of 65,941 miles an hour—the spacecraft, while moving 25,700 miles an hour slower than Earth, would thus be moving at a net speed of 40,249 miles an hour around the Sun. At this lesser speed it would be unable to maintain the same orbit as Earth's, and as a consequence would begin falling inward in a gentle elliptical curve toward the Sun and toward the orbit of Venus. During the first three days of flight, its speed away from and in relation to Earth would be slowed by Earth's gravity from 25,700 miles an hour to approximately one quarter of that. The spacecraft would then be approximately 600,000 miles from Earth. Twenty days after that, the spacecraft would be approximately 3.5 million miles away from Earth. At this point the influence of Earth's gravity which, although ever-present, would have declined steadily since launch, would be counterbalanced by the ever-present and steadily increasing gravitational pull of the Sun, and the speed of Mariner 2 in relation to Earth would begin to increase. As the spacecraft continued to fall inward toward the Sun, its speed would continue increasing, and in time it would catch up with and overtake Earth while travelling along the elliptical trajectory that had been calculated to bring it to the vicinity of Venus on the date of encounter.

After injection into its interplanetary transfer orbit and separation from the Agena second stage, Mariner 2 was travelling in space in a gently tumbling motion caused by the act of separation, and with its solar panels still folded up in their launch position. Forty-four minutes after launch, the first of a series of commands was automatically issued from within the spacecraft. The solar panels were released by pyrotechnic devices—explosive pin-pullers—from locks holding them in their launch position against the conical sides of the spacecraft; and the panels, which were spring-loaded at their base, slowly folded outward and downward to lock in their cruise positions. In the process, and according to plan, the microwave radiometer, to which was affixed the infrared radiometer, was freed from a latch holding it to its particular launch position. However, the radiometer was not scheduled to be used until the time of Venus encounter.

The signal to carry out these motions was issued by an internal control center aboard the spacecraft called the Central Computer and Sequencer (C.C. & S.). The function of the C.C. & S. is to provide computations for various subsystems of the spacecraft and to issue commands to these subsystems in a predetermined sequence. These commands are stored in the C.C. & S. not in the form of magnetic tape or any such familiar device, but in the form of a complex of electronic switches, the operation of which is governed by an electronic clock.

Sixty minutes after launch, the C.C. & S. issued its next command affecting the behavior of the spacecraft. It turned on the attitude control system, and began the process of orienting the spacecraft to the Sun. The attitude control system is a stabilizing system for controlling the posture (as distinct from the direction of flight) of the spacecraft while in its interplanetary path. The stabilization is provided by the action of the ten small gas jets mounted about the spacecraft, and fed from small bottles of nitrogen. Their operation is electrically linked to three gyros within the attitude control system, to the Earth sensor attached to the directional antenna, and to six Sun sensors mounted on the hexagonal base of the spacecraft and on the backs of the solar panels. These Sun sensors are photoelectric cells sensitive to the light of the Sun. As, in the darkness of space, sunlight falls upon them, the circuitry attached to the Sun sensors measures the extent to which the spacecraft is properly oriented to the Sun. When the spacecraft is not properly oriented to the Sun, the attitude control system informs the gyros and gas jets of this condition. The gas jets, using the gyros for reference, then maneuver the spacecraft in the necessary motions of roll, pitch, and yaw until the proper orientation to the Sun is established. The gas in the small tanks, although it is contained under tremendous pressure, is squirted in short bursts out of the jets (the nozzles of which are almost pinhole size) quite gently —so gently that anybody examining the action of one of these jets before the spacecraft left the ground would have had to put his hand within about eight inches of the nozzle to feel any pressure against it—but in the weightless conditions of space these jets maneuver the spacecraft about quite easily until it settles into its proper attitude.

One hour after launch, upon command from the C.C. & S., the attitude control system, with its jets and gyros, cancelled out the tumbling motion of Mariner 2 and oriented the spacecraft so that the apex of its conical frame was pointing directly at the Sun. However, it did not interfere at this stage with the freely rolling motion of the spacecraft about its long axis; that is, about the line running from the apex of the cone through the middle of the base. The attitude control system then turned the gyros off and held the spacecraft to its Sun-oriented position. When the spacecraft had thus locked on to, or acquired, the Sun, the panels of solar cells extending out from the base were squarely exposed to the Sun, and they began converting solar energy into electricity. The spacecraft, which up to now had been drawing its power from a rechargeable battery on board, began to use the solar panels as its main source of power; henceforth the battery would be used only when the solar panels were not supplying adequate power.

Two days after launch the spacecraft received a radio command from the Deep Space Instrumentation Facility tracking station at Johannesburg that caused a subsystem to turn on four of the six scientific experiments on board: the magnetometer and the charged-particle detector, the solar plasma detector and cosmic dust detector. As the sensors for these four experiments set to work making measurements of various conditions, the measurements were periodically encoded by a data-conditioning system and communicated back to Earth through the omni-antenna. According to plan, the spacecraft would continue making and transmitting these measurements for the remainder of the mission except during an approaching midcourse maneuver.

The next major command affecting the behavior of the spacecraft was issued by the C.C. & S. seven days after launch, when the spacecraft was 1.2 million miles from Earth. At 3:29 A. M. on September 3, the C.C. & S. started a sequence of events that would enable the spacecraft's high-gain, or directional, antenna, which was designed for communication with Earth from great interplanetary distances, to seek out the position of Earth and to lock on to it until further command. The scientific instruments were turned off and the gyros were turned on. The Earth sensor attached to the directional antenna was also turned on. The Earth sensor consists of an optical telescope and a series of light-sensitive cells. Its function is to inform the attitude control system of the extent to which it is perceiving the Earth's light; the attitude control system, with its jets, sees to it that the spacecraft is kept in such an attitude that the Earth remains in view of the sensor.

When the Earth sensor was turned on and the Earth acquisition process began, the spacecraft remained in a Sun-oriented attitude, but as yet it was still rolling freely about its long axis, with the solar panels slowly revolving like the arms of a windmill pointed at the Sun. This gentle rolling of the spacecraft now was taken advantage of for the purpose of enabling the Earth sensor mounted on the directional antenna to slew around in the manner of a radar antenna and to seek out the position of Earth.

Very shortly the Earth sensor indicated to the attitude control system that Earth had entered its view. The attitude control system then slowed the spacecraft's roll until the Earth sensor and the directional radio antenna to which it was attached were—presumably—locked on Earth.

As it might be seen from the position of Mariner 2 in space, Earth at this time was about two-thirds the size of the Moon as the Moon might be seen, full, from Earth. Viewed from the position of the spacecraft, the condition of Earth was gibbous—slightly more than half the planetary disc was illuminated—with the terminator, the plane dividing the sunlit from the dark side, running roughly along the international date line. The major land areas in view were China, Indonesia, Australia, and Wilkes Land in Antarctica. The Sun had set on Midway and Samoa, and was about to set on Wellington, New Zealand. India was coming into view and it was high noon in East Pakistan. The Moon, about one third of the size of Earth as the two bodies might be seen from the spacecraft, lay to the right of Earth and downward about ten degrees below Earth's equator.

When the Earth sensor had settled into a position which the attitude control system accepted as being in lock with the image of Earth, the spacecraft's communication with Earth was transferred from the omni-antenna to the long-range directional antenna. The Earth acquisition maneuver was completed 33 minutes after it started, and upon its completion the C.C. & S. turned the gyros off and switched the scientific experiments on again.

The spacecraft was now established in its cruise mode, a dual orientation to Sun and Earth that, with the exception of the period of the midcourse maneuver, it was designed to maintain for the rest of the mission. The scheduled time for the midcourse maneuver, by means of which the flight path of the spacecraft was to be modified slightly so as to bring it in closer contact with Venus, was approaching. According to studies made by tracking stations on Earth since the time of launch, it had been calculated that without a midcourse correction Mariner 2 would make its closest approach to Venus on December 13, a day earlier than the flight plan called for, at 3:30 P.M., at a point 233,000 miles from the planet. Computations were now made of the corrections necessary to bring the spacecraft to within the original target area, between 10,000 and 35,000 miles off the Sunward side of Venus, and to bring it there at the original estimated time of arrival on December 14.

According to the flight plan, the maneuver involved in the midcourse correction was supposed to take place on the evening of September 3, but as a result of ambiguous information that Mariner 2 was sending back to Earth about its condition, the maneuver was postponed. The difficulty lay with the data being reported by the spacecraft on the functioning of the Earth sensor, the reading of which indicated that the Earth sensor might have locked itself on to the Moon rather than the Earth. At the same time, the reading of the angle at which the directional antenna of the spacecraft was pointing indicated that the Earth sensor was locked on Earth rather than on the Moon. To resolve this question, the midcourse maneuver was put off so that telemetry data from the spacecraft could be studied. By the morning of September 4 it was decided that the Earth sensor was indeed locked on Earth and not on the Moon.

The midcourse maneuver got under way that morning during the period when the spacecraft was in radio view of the Goldstone tracking station. Between 9:30 A.M. and 10:23 P.M. Goldstone sent three radio commands to the spacecraft concerning changes of attitude and velocity that

would be required to put it on its correct trajectory to
Venus. Each of the commands contained a code instructing
the C.C. & S. to hold the commands in electronic storage.
At 10:39 P.M. Goldstone then sent what is known as a
"real-time command" (as distinct from a command intended
for storage, which is known as a "stored-time command")
to the spacecraft to switch its transmitting power from the
directional antenna to the omni-antenna, and ten minutes
later another command followed instructing the C.C. & S.
to set the midcourse maneuver in motion.

Upon receipt of this last command aboard the
spacecraft, the working scientific experiments were turned
off and the gyros were turned on. The gyros were allowed
to warm up for an hour. Then the spacecraft turned off
the Earth sensor, and using the gyros as orienting references,
began a roll turn of 9.33 degrees with the aid of the gas
jets. At the same time the C.C. & S. instructed the hinge-
mounted directional antenna to move out of the path of the
midcourse rocket-motor exhaust.

Eleven minutes after the beginning of the roll
turn, and on the first second of September 5, the C.C. & S.
turned off the Sun sensors, and the spacecraft, its attitude
now being guided by its gyros, began a pitch turn of 139.83
degrees. As the pitch turn progressed, the solar panels
heeled over from their normal orientation to the Sun, upon
which the storage battery took over the job of supplying
all of the power needed by the spacecraft.

In 23 minutes the pitch turn was completed. The
spacecraft, temporarily deprived of the use of its Sun and
Earth sensors, now was held by its gyros in the attitude
that put it in readiness for the firing of the midcourse rocket
motor. The midcourse motor, set in the base of the space-

ALONE *THROUGH THE DARK SEA* | 154

craft, is a comparatively small affair propelled by liquid hydrazine fuel. It is designed for such precise operation that it is capable of increasing the velocity of the spacecraft by such small amounts as seven and a quarter inches a second.

The velocity change that Goldstone had instructed the spacecraft to give itself by means of the midcourse motor was an increase of 69.5 miles an hour, the intended effect of this change upon the trajectory being to divert the spacecraft's path very slightly outward, in relation to the Sun, from its existing one, and very slightly lower in its arch over the ecliptic.

The midcourse motor was ignited at 12:23 A.M. and, for the purpose of increasing the velocity of the spacecraft to the required amount, it burned for 28.7 seconds. Four and a half minutes after the motor was turned off the Sun sensors were turned on again, and the spacecraft began reorienting itself to the Sun. At the same time the directional antenna was retracted to its previous position, the Earth sensor reacquired the Earth, the directional antenna began working again, and the midcourse maneuver was completed.

Mariner 2 was back in its cruise mode, the apex of its conical superstructure pointed at the Sun, its directional antenna pointed at Earth. As it had been before the midcourse maneuver, it was travelling in a motion that had three components. As it might have been seen from above the celestial sphere, it was travelling, like Earth, counterclockwise around the Sun. It was falling inward toward the Sun and the orbit of Venus. And it was travelling in a direction slightly upward over the ecliptic. But now, all three components of its motion had been so modi-

fied by the midcourse maneuver that, according to preliminary computations on the ground, its changed path
was expected to place the spacecraft within 9,000 miles of
the Sunward side of Venus at the time of closest approach
on December 14. The speed of the spacecraft was estimated
to have changed to an extent that can be expressed in two
ways: relative to the speed of Earth the speed of Mariner 2
had decreased by 59 miles an hour, to 6,689 miles an hour;
relative to the Sun, its speed had increased by 45 miles an
hour, to 60,162 miles an hour.

Having completed the midcourse maneuver, Mariner 2 was now travelling in a position 1,492,500 miles
behind Earth in Earth's motion around the Sun and approximately 7,000 miles inward from Earth's path. In the
eight days since launch, Earth had travelled 11 million miles
forward in its slightly elliptical path around the Sun;
Mariner 2, trailing behind Earth in its own and more
elliptical path around the Sun, had travelled 8.5 million
miles. The spacecraft, having long since recovered from its
initial dip below the ecliptic when it was first injected into
space, had risen above that invisible plane between the
center of the Earth and Sun and now was travelling at a
point 421,300 miles above the ecliptic. Later, as it progressed, it would arch even farther above the ecliptic to a
maximum altitude of 2.4 million miles above it before
gradually falling downward again until, after crossing the
path of Venus, it would sink below the ecliptic and continue
around the Sun.

The orbit of the spacecraft might be visualized by
superimposing, on a Sun-centered model of the great outer
wheel of Earth's path and the inner wheel of Venus's path
(each path being a slightly elliptical one and being tilted

at a slight angle to the other), a third and quite off-centered wheel, tilted at yet another slightly different angle. This third elliptical wheel would be so placed that part of it would lie athwart and touch the rims of the two other wheels—the outer path of Earth and the inner path of Venus. It is between these points of contact and along such a slightly tilted, markedly elliptical rim that the trajectory of Mariner 2 between launch and encounter would extend. Computations of the spacecraft's position and speed immediately after midcourse indicated that on the projected encounter date 101 days hence Venus would be 173.5 million miles distant from the present position of the spacecraft. It was further computed that the spacecraft's closest approach to Venus, on December 14, would occur at 5:45 P.M.

After the midcourse maneuver, Mariner 2 cruised without incident in Sun and Earth lock for four days, continuously transmitting scientific information and engineering data on its own performance. Then on September 8, the twelfth day of flight, at 12:30 P.M., the gyros started up and ran for three minutes, indicating that the spacecraft had departed from its prescribed attitude. Precisely what happened during that period is unknown, but it is thought that the spacecraft was struck by a micrometeorite and was momentarily deflected from its Sun and Earth lock. Whatever the cause, the disturbance appeared to have no ill effects on the operation of the spacecraft.

But, unlike this disturbance, another unusual condition that had developed aboard the spacecraft since the seventh day after launch had not cleared up and presented a potential hazard to the entire mission. Ever since the moment that the spacecraft had gone through its Earth-locking maneuver, its engineering data had been indicating that the Earth sensor was showing far less sensitivity to light than it should. It was this abnormality that had caused concern on the ground at the time of Earth acquisition as to whether the Earth sensor was locked on the Moon instead of the more luminous Earth, and now the possibility arose that as the spacecraft moved farther away from Earth the Earth sensor would lose its ability to hold its optical lock on the Earth, in which case the usefulness of the mission would be seriously impaired. Through nearly all of September the sensitivity of the Earth sensor as indicated by telemetry continued to drop until, by September 29, it was very near the point at which it could no longer be measured. Then, shortly after noon on that day, the gyros of the spacecraft came on again briefly—whether another micrometeorite impact caused this new disturbance nobody knows —whereupon telemetry showed that the Earth sensor had somehow suddenly healed itself of its apparent malfunction. While the spacecraft continued on its interplanetary voyage, the measurements being periodically transmitted back to Earth on the sensitivity of the optical Earth sensor showed clear variations in brightness readings from one period of a day to another as, on the revolving Earth, oceans and land masses slowly alternated in the sensor's field of view.

On September 18, approximately midway between the dates of the two disturbances, the spacecraft, the speed of which relative to Earth had been steadily decreasing since launch owing to Earth's gravitational influence upon it, reached its lowest Earth-relative speed of 6,448.3 miles an hour at a point 3.5 million miles behind and inward from Earth in Earth's path around the Sun. At this same point, the spacecraft began to increase its speed relative to Earth as the spacecraft followed its inward-turning path toward the orbit of Venus. By October 5, a month after the midcourse maneuver, Mariner 2 had increased its Earth-related speed to 6,976 miles an hour and its speed relative to the Sun to 64,310 miles an hour. After a month of intensive tracking by the Deep Space Instrumentation Facility, the effects of the midcourse maneuver on the spacecraft's trajectory could be computed with more accuracy than at the completion of the actual maneuver. According to such new computations, the midcourse maneuver was now shown to have somehow increased the spacecraft's velocity by 72 miles an hour rather than the 69.5 miles an hour planned, or an extra 2.5 miles an hour on top of a desired total speed relative to the Sun of 60,162 miles an hour. As a result, the trajectory of the spacecraft was calculated to have been altered sufficiently so as to place Mariner 2, at its projected closest approach to Venus, well within the target area but at a position approximately 20,900 miles instead of 9,000 miles on the Sunward side of the planet, and at 8 P.M. instead of 5:45 P.M., as expected, on December 14.

Along this trajectory the spacecraft continued in its cruise attitude without further incident through all but the last day of October. Its four scientific experiments were still turned on, and measurements from the experiments were being encoded by the data-conditioning system and were being transmitted to Earth by the directional antenna through millions of miles of interplanetary space—or what might be properly called the "interplanetary medium," for, as the spacecraft's scientific instruments were showing, what Mariner 2 was travelling through was not sheer empty space, but an ocean of nuclear plasma borne on the solar wind. While the solar wind was a very thin one—its density amounted only to about 10 to 20 low-energy charged particles per cubic inch—it never ceased flowing outward from the Sun, and the velocity of its particles was never lower than 200 miles a second. Sometimes, as the instruments aboard the spacecraft showed, the ever-flowing solar wind turned gusty, with squalls of 500 miles a second— twenty such squalls were measured at various times during the voyage—and when these gusts occurred, the spacecraft's instruments showed that they pushed around magnetic fields in space. And measurement of these periods of turmoil in space served as advance warnings of storms that later occurred in Earth's magnetic field. Geiger-Müller tubes aboard Mariner 2 also counted, as the voyage progressed, the rate of cosmic rays penetrating the solar system from galactic space. The collection of this data has made it possible to conclude, for the first time, that under conditions similar to those prevailing during the Mariner 2 mission, the danger to astronauts from cosmic radiation during future manned interplanetary voyages will not be great.

Not long after the midcourse maneuver, ground tracking information had made it reasonably certain that the spacecraft was travelling along a trajectory that would take it to the target area off Venus as previously calculated. But whether it would still be in proper working order by the time it reached the vicinity of the planet was another matter. On October 31, the sixty-fifth day of flight, the spacecraft, having steadily increased its orbital speed, came abreast of Earth in Earth's motion around the Sun—it was a "full" Earth as visible to the Earth sensor—and passed it at a distance of 11.5 million miles and at a heliocentric speed 4,741 miles an hour greater than Earth's. At 5:30 A.M. on that day, the voltage being generated by each of the solar panels suddenly dropped to a serious extent; telemetry indicated that one of the panels had developed a short circuit, had ceased to function, and was draining power from the other working panel. As a consequence, as telemetry showed, the spacecraft was approaching a condition in which it was about to draw upon power from its battery. Since the spacecraft still had 43 days and approximately 40 million miles to go before reaching Venus, any depletion of the battery at this stage of flight involved certain risk to a vital reserve. To reduce this risk and to conserve power aboard the spacecraft for some time, the tracking station at Goldstone later that day sent out a special command that turned off the scientific experiments aboard the spacecraft. Mariner 2 continued in its cruise attitude. In the first week of November, it picked up speed, in accordance with the computed trajectory characteristics, at a sharply increased rate along its now increasingly inward-turning path toward the Sun and the orbit of Venus. As it came closer to the Sun, the cells of the one working solar panel were able to draw enough extra energy from the Sun to compensate for some of the loss caused by the short circuit. By November 8, when the spacecraft had travelled 12.7 million miles along its trajectory and come 2.6 million miles Sunward since the short circuit, Goldstone prepared to send a command to turn the scientific instruments on again, but before the command was sent, the short circuit on the solar panel suddenly cleared up.

The spacecraft continued in its cruise attitude for another week without incident. Then, on November 15, the eightieth day of flight, the short circuit in the faulty solar panel reappeared. However, by this time the effect of the short circuit was not too injurious, for the spacecraft was now drawing so much closer to the Sun that a correspondingly greater amount of solar energy striking the solar panels was providing enough electricity to compensate for most of the accidental power loss. As a consequence, the scientific experiments, rather than being turned off as before by ground command as a power-conserving measure, were kept functioning.

The spacecraft, the motion and course of which in the last ten days or so had been increasingly affected by the gravitational influence of Venus as well as that of the Sun, was now travelling at greatly increased speed. On November 21, travelling at a heliocentric speed of 77,289 miles an hour, it reached the top of its trajectory arch over the ecliptic. As the spacecraft passed the top of the arch the invisible plane of the ecliptic lay 2.4 million miles below it; along that plane Earth, now travelling well behind the spacecraft, lay at a point 20.28 million miles away. Venus, travelling in its inner path around the Sun at a speed yet greater than that of the spacecraft, was still below the ecliptic, but was closely approaching it as it moved upward along its slightly sloping path. A week later, on November 28, Venus, having travelled, since the time of launch, 150 million miles from a position 2.3 million miles below the ecliptic, made its ecliptic passage at a distance of 7.4 million miles from the spacecraft. As Venus ascended in its path through the ecliptic, the spacecraft continued its descent from the top of its arching path and toward the ecliptic. By December 1 the spacecraft, now travelling at the rate of 1.9 million miles a day, was 25.9 million miles away from the point where its path was calculated to intersect the orbit of Venus.

Mariner 2 now had moved sufficiently close to the

Sun that the increase in solar energy which the working solar panel was converting into electricity was almost entirely compensating for the power loss caused by the short circuit in the faulty solar panel. But as the spacecraft moved ever closer to the Sun the increased solar energy that was resolving this power problem was also creating a very serious problem of a different kind. Engineering data being transmitted to Earth by the directional antenna indicated that the temperatures of various working components of the spacecraft were rising very close to or actually above the point at which these components were designed to operate.

The problem of maintaining temperatures aboard a spacecraft such as Mariner 2 within specified bounds under the conditions prevailing during various phases of flight is a complex one. Various parts of the spacecraft are subjected during the mission to great temperature extremes. In order that its components be kept within temperature ranges that will allow them to operate properly during flight, the spacecraft is designed to absorb, reflect, and radiate heat in a precisely balanced manner. Its metal parts are polished to a carefully calculated degree of reflectivity. Electronic equipment clustered around the base of the spacecraft is insulated, on the side which is fully exposed to the Sun when the spacecraft is in its Sun-oriented attitude, by temperature shields covered with layers of aluminum-coated plastic, and on the side of the hexagon that remains in the dark during Sun orientation by a second shield designed to prevent undue loss of heat into space from heat generated internally by the operation of the electronic control equipment. The temperature of the attitude control subsystem is designed to be kept in bounds by polished aluminum louvers. In addition to these devices, the spacecraft is also equipped with various thermal control shields and radiators made of thin gold plate and aluminum sheeting, and parts of exposed surfaces were also covered with complex paint patterns. The thermal balance of the Mariner 2 was sufficiently delicate that, in its design, even a slight improper variation in the balance of a paint pattern could mean the difference between a component freezing or burning up during the mission; indeed, this calculated balance was so fine that it could be upset even by the presence of fingerprints on exposed surfaces, and during the manufacture of the spacecraft special precautions were taken in this regard.

Despite these elaborate precautions, the temperatures of various components, as Mariner 2 travelled through millions of miles in interplanetary space, turned out to be higher than expected, and by the first week in December the temperatures of some made it appear questionable whether several vital components would continue working properly until the spacecraft reached its target. For example, the battery was becoming seriously overheated, and the possibility even arose that, if overheated sufficiently, it might explode. Furthermore, the light sensitivity of the optical Earth sensor was being adversely affected by the increased temperatures, and even though this loss in sensitivity might have been partly offset by a certain slight seasonal increase in the reflectivity of Earth as perceptible from the spacecraft, owing to the coming of winter snows and increased cloud cover in the Northern Hemisphere, there was no guaranteeing that the Earth sensor would hold out until the crucial hour of encounter.

In the meantime the spacecraft continued along a course very close to its altered trajectory, and the paths

of Mariner 2 and the planet now began to draw comparatively close together, with Venus still ascending out of the
ecliptic and the spacecraft still descending toward the ecliptic in their respective orbital motions around the Sun. The
angles of ascent and descent were very slight—for Venus 1.4
degrees, for the spacecraft 1.9 degrees; but because of the
scale involved, the distances travelled upward and downward were considerable, more than a hundred thousand
miles a day for each body.

By December 10 the spacecraft, still maintaining
in its cruise mode its Sun and Earth lock and still satisfactorily transmitting scientific and engineering telemetry,
reached a heliocentric speed of 83,253 miles an hour along
its trajectory, and a point 1.3 million miles distant from
steadily-ascending Venus, which lay somewhat ahead of it
in its path and at an angle downward from it of approximately 28 degrees. At this time Venus, as it might be seen
from the spacecraft, was about three-quarters of the size
of the Moon as the Moon might be seen, full, from Earth.
(As perceivable from the position of the spacecraft, about
a quarter of the surface of Venus was in sunlight.)

By 6 A.M. on December 12, as the path of the
spacecraft curved increasingly inward, the distance between
the spacecraft and Venus decreased to 783,146 miles, and
by noon on December 13 the distance had decreased to
414,296 miles. The spacecraft, having come under the pre-
dominant gravitational influence of Venus, was now in the
Cytherean phase of its interplanetary trajectory.

By 6 A.M. on December 14, the day of predicted
encounter, the distance between the spacecraft and Venus
decreased further to 192,015 miles, at which point Venus

lay 27 degrees below the spacecraft. Mariner 2, travelling at a heliocentric speed of 84,481 miles an hour, was gaining rapidly on Venus as its descending path turned yet further inward toward the Sun and toward the ascending path of Venus, and by 6 A.M. only 81 minutes remained before the time when the central computer and sequencer, acting on instructions fed into it just prior to launch 109 days previously, was due to issue an internal command that would turn on the radiometer experiments and cause the spacecraft to change from its cruise mode to its planetary encounter mode.

The spacecraft was equipped with the radiometers for the purpose of determining accurately the nature of the atmosphere of Venus and the temperatures prevailing at and above its surface. The principal instrument of the planetary experiments, the microwave radiometer, consisted of a motor-driven device somewhat like a searchlight in appearance (actually it was a small parabolic antenna) that was designed to scan the surface of Venus and detect any electromagnetic radiation emanating from the planet in two wave lengths. One wave length, 13.5 millimeters, represents a band in the microwave region, capable of reflecting the presence of water vapor, and the radiometer was made sensitive to this wave length so that data from it, combined with data from another wave length, 19 millimeters, which is not in the water vapor band, would be capable of providing indications as to whether or not the atmosphere of Venus contains water vapor in any great amount. The radiometer's 19-millimeter channel was designed to register radiation from the surface of the planet and also to provide information on whether the high-temperature measurements of the atmosphere of Venus were truly due to surface conditions or, as had been suggested, were merely the result of distortions caused by a very dense ionosphere on Venus.

To provide this information, the radiometer was designed to scan the surface of the planet in such a way as to detect one of two planetary conditions known as limb brightening or limb darkening. The limb of Venus is the edge of its planetary disc. As this disc, supposing it were to be covered with a fine mist, might be seen by an observer placed a few thousand miles away, the concentration of mist would appear thicker toward its edge than at the center, because as the observer's gaze might travel from the center toward the limb, he would be looking through an increasing amount of atmosphere owing to the curvature of the planet's surface. In a somewhat similar way, the radiometer was designed to scan, or gaze across, the cloud-covered surface of the planet, and as it scanned across it from, say, the center to the edge, it would encounter and register an increasingly thicker concentration of atmosphere. If, upon its approach to the edge during its scan, the temperatures it was measuring decreased, a limb darkening would be observed, and the radiometer data would indicate that the high temperatures definitely were those at the surface. If, however, the temperatures were to increase just as the scan swept off the planetary disc, the source of the high temperatures could be interpreted as atmospheric, and it might be possible then to tell, by crossing the radiometer data with other collected data, whether they were due to the existence of a dense ionosphere.

The infrared radiometer, an instrument six inches long and two inches wide, which was rigidly attached to and aligned with the microwave radiometer, was designed as a

companion to the microwave experiment. Like the microwave radiometer, it was a dual channel instrument. One
channel was designed to scan the cloud cover of Venus; the
other was designed to detect the presence of carbon dioxide
in the atmosphere. If there were no breaks in the cloud
cover, the relationship between the readings of both the
cloud-scanning channel and the carbon-dioxide-scanning
channel would remain constant; if there were breaks in the
cover, the cloud-scanning channel readings would be different from those of the carbon dioxide scan. And, again,
if there were cloud breaks, a matching of the microwave
radiometer data would indicate the temperature of whatever heat might be escaping through the breaks into space.
In this and other ways, the information collected by the
four channels of the two experiments was expected to be
correlated so as to provide a fairly detailed picture of the
atmospheric and surface conditions of the planet.

The microwave radiometer, with its infrared radiometer attached to it, was mounted on a support capable of
swivelling it vertically when the spacecraft was in its cruise
attitude. According to pre-launch instructions, the central
computer and sequencer was supposed to activate the radiometer experiments and to put the spacecraft into its encounter mode at 7:21 A.M., ten hours before the time of
encounter as that time had been estimated prior to launch.

However, when that time at last arrived, nothing
happened. The functioning of the C.C. & S. was impaired by
the rising temperatures within the spacecraft. Fortunately,
the C.C. & S. was so designed that if it did not issue or put
into effect the "begin encounter" command at the pro-
grammed instant, it would automatically issue the same

command once more after an interval of three hours and 20 seconds.

At 10:41 A.M. Greenwich Mean Time on December 14, therefore, when the spacecraft reached a position 130,000 miles from Venus and 20 degrees above it, the time for the second internal command arrived. But again no internal signal was forthcoming from the C.C. & S., and telemetry from the spacecraft showed that no change in its condition had taken place.

However, this further eventuality also had been foreseen during the design stage of the spacecraft, and provisions had been made for a "begin encounter" sequence to be activated, if all other means failed, by a ground command that would bypass the C.C. & S. At 1:35 P.M., when the spacecraft was in radio view of the Goldstone tracking station, the ground command was sent in real, or, rather, in near-real time, because, travelling at the rate of 186,000 miles a second, the speed of light, the signal took 188 seconds to reach the spacecraft from Earth. Six and a quarter minutes after the signal left Earth, a signal from the spacecraft verifying the reception of the command reached Earth; at 1:38 P.M. in near-real time the spacecraft was successfully switched into its encounter mode with all its scientific experiments, including the radiometers, working, and its engineering data collecting mechanism turned off. At the moment of their activation, the microwave and infrared radiometers, driven by a small motor, began to move on their common support in a scanning or nodding motion, up and down at the rate of one degree a second in search for the planet. Their area of search lay to the right in the direction of flight. The radiometers continued in this scanning motion for five hours and twenty minutes.

By 2 P.M., as the Sunward-turning course of the descending spacecraft curved in toward the Sun-encircling course of ascending Venus, the spacecraft was gaining on Venus, in relation to the orbital speed of the planet, at the rate of 13,120 miles an hour. The planet lay 20 degrees below the spacecraft and to the right of the path in which the spacecraft was travelling, at a distance of 79,886 miles. About a quarter of its visible surface was in sunlight, the bright area extending in a crescent around the left side and over the north polar region. The planet as it might have been seen from the spacecraft was approximately ten times the size of the full Moon as seen from Earth.

Two hours later the spacecraft, travelling at 13,492 miles an hour in relation to Venus, was 55,556 miles distant from it. The angle between the positions of the ascending planet and the descending spacecraft was only 11 degrees, and the size of Venus, from the spacecraft, was fourteen times the size of the Moon as seen from Earth. By 5 P.M., the spacecraft was 43,907 miles away, and the angle at which it lay above Venus had shrunk to six degrees. By 6 P.M. Mariner 2, at a distance of 33,183 miles from the planet, had descended to a level three degrees below the center of Venus.

Then, at 6:55 P.M., the coupled radiometers, in their scan up and down of the void of space, encountered the edge of Venus on its dark side at a distance of 25,257 miles. When they did so, the radiometer mechanism automatically changed the rate of its nodding motion from one degree a second to one tenth of one degree a second, and began measuring the surface, atmosphere, and cloud cover of the planet. Simultaneously, the other scientific experiments that had been working during the cruise period of the mission were carrying out their functions: the magnetometer was taking magnetic field measurements of the planetary area; the ion chamber and radiation counters were measuring the intensity and distribution of charged particles and were looking for evidence of a Van Allen radiation belt around Venus; the solar plasma detector was measuring the flow and density of the solar wind and the energy of its particles; and the cosmic dust detector was ready to count cosmic dust particles. And the spacecraft was transmitting information from these experiments to Earth through 35.9 million miles of interplanetary space, with its full radio power of less than 3 watts, the equivalent of the power produced by the two small cells of an ordinary flashlight.

At 7:16 P.M. the spacecraft, travelling in an in-increasingly downward direction across and behind Venus in the path of the planet around the Sun, passed the terminator, the line dividing the light from the dark side of the planet, at a speed of 14,935 miles an hour in relation to Venus, the position of the spacecraft being 22 degrees below the level of the center of Venus. The orbital paths of the two heavenly bodies, the paths of the descending spacecraft and ascending Venus, were then intersected at a point 1.6 million miles above the great invisible wheel of the ecliptic.

Twenty minutes later the radiometers completed their survey of the planet, and at 7:59 P.M. the spacecraft made its closest approach to Venus on its sunlit side at a distance of 21,648 miles from the surface and at an angle of 36 degrees below the center of the planet. As it might have been seen from the spacecraft, Venus was now 33 times bigger than the full Moon as seen from Earth. Earth itself, as it might have been seen from the spacecraft, would be about as big as Venus would appear from Earth in the evening sky, but—because it is farther away from the Sun than Venus and has a far less dense atmosphere—less than half as bright.

In the 109.5 days since launch, Earth, moving in its path around the Sun, had travelled 285 million miles, and owing to the slight eccentricity of its path, was now 2.4 million miles closer to the Sun, and was travelling at a heliocentric speed of 1,673 miles an hour faster than at the time of launch. Venus, in its nearly circular path around the Sun, had travelled 328 million miles, had come 8,143 miles closer to the Sun, and was moving 965 miles an hour faster around it than it was at launch-time owing to its proximity to the Sun. And the spacecraft, having been fired from a terrestrial body moving at an orbital speed of 65,914 miles an hour toward a planetary target moving at 88,126 miles an hour at a distance of 180.9 million miles, had arrived within its specified target area and made its closest approach to Venus one minute ahead of the encounter time predicted more than two months earlier.

The scientific information collected by Mariner 2 during its period of encounter with Venus is under intensive study, and the drawing of conclusions from this data is a process that will certainly go on for years, for what is fundamentally involved is knowledge not only of Venus itself but of the nature and origin of the solar system and its relationship to other systems of matter in galactic space. Thus far analysis of the Mariner data has yielded, with a relatively high degree of certainty, a number of facts about Venus. The planet is found to have, on both its light and dark sides, a fairly uniform surface temperature of about 800 degrees Fahrenheit, which makes the existence of any life on or near its surface a virtual impossibility. No holes were detected in the dense cloud cover, which has an average thickness of about 15 miles and lies at an altitude of between 45 and 60 miles above the surface. The clouds are composed not primarily of water (Venus appears to possess only one-thousandth of the concentration of water found on Earth) but probably of condensed hydrocarbons, so that the cloud layer has the texture of a very thick oily smog. It is probable that only a little reddish light filters through this cloud layer to the surface. The temperature at the base of the clouds is quite high, about 200 degrees, but at the top of the clouds it is very low by Earth standards, between 60 and 70 degrees below zero. The only temperature irregularity was measured in an area at the south end of the terminator, and may have been caused by the presence there of a very high montain the top of which was hidden in the clouds. This mountain, if it exists, would be at least 45 miles high.

The planetary scan by the radiometers revealed, among other things, a limb darkening, which indicates that Venus does not have a dense ionosphere. The high temperatures at the surface of the planet thus are probably due to the "greenhouse" effect caused by the trapping of solar heat under the cloud cover. Unlike Earth, Venus was found to have no radiation belt around it, at least in the areas traversed by Mariner 2, and the magnetometer aboard the spacecraft detected no planetary magnetic field. (This does not mean that Venus does not possess a magnetic field, but only that if this field exists, it does not extend to the altitudes penetrated by the spacecraft.)

Besides providing this information, Mariner 2, by sending periodic signals that made possible computation of its velocity away from Earth to an accuracy of one-tenth of an inch per second, provided a good deal of important information concerning astronomical distances. Up to the present, our knowledge of the layout of the solar system has been something like a blueprint in which the proportions of one part to another are accurately represented, but in which the scale of the drawing to the original is not very accurately known. By providing data that enabled its speed to be measured accurately, Mariner 2 also provided an accurate measure of the distances it travelled. Thus, for example, its data makes possible a further refinement of the Astronomical Unit, or the mean distance between the Sun and Earth. Also, measurement of the perturbation of the spacecraft's trajectory by the gravitational force of Venus during the period of encounter—the position of the spacecraft in relation to Venus during that period is known to an accuracy of 10 miles—has made it possible to determine with new accuracy the mass of Venus. Data from the spacecraft can also be used to make a new and more accurate determination of the mass of the Moon, and even the precise location of the Deep Space tracking stations on Earth. (Before the Mariner 2 mission, the precise geographical location of the Goldstone station had been known to within 100 yards; Mariner 2 data will permit its position on the Earth's surface to be computed to an accuracy of 20 yards.)

After its encounter with Venus on December 14, Mariner 2 continued in its cruise mode along a path sufficiently altered by the gravitational influence of Venus that twelve days later it lay approximately 1.3 million miles farther away from the Sun than it would have been had it continued on the path it had been taking before its approach to Venus. Its path was also deflected slightly upward by Venus, so that instead of continuing its descent toward the ecliptic Mariner 2 was temporarily ascending away from it. On December 27, the spacecraft, still correctly orienting itself to Sun and Earth, and still transmitting scientific and engineering data to Earth, made its perihelion passage, or closest orbital approach to the Sun, at a distance of 65.5 million miles, and it continued in its Venus-influenced path above the ecliptic.

Then, on January 3, the one-hundred-thirtieth day of flight, at 6 P.M., radio contact with Mariner 2 was lost. When it was last heard from, the spacecraft lay 1.9 million miles above the ecliptic at a distance of 53.8 million miles from Earth and at a distance of 5.6 million miles from and beyond Venus and it was travelling at a heliocentric speed of 89,141 miles an hour in its elliptical orbit around the Sun. That orbit is describable, in the coldly elegant language of astronomy, by its orbital elements: the semi-major axis and the eccentricity of its conic section; its inclination to the ecliptic; the longitude of the ascending node; the argument of perihelion; the time of perihelion passage. The orbit of the spacecraft, subject only to possible slight distortion by the solar wind, is a perpetual one.